Mac Design
Out of the Box

Andrew Shalat

Mac Design Out of the Box

Andrew Shalat

Inside Mac is published in association with Pearson Education

Pearson Education
1249 Eighth Street
Berkeley, CA 94710
510/524-2178
800/283-9444
510/524-2221 (fax)

Find us on the World Wide Web at: www.peachpit.com
To report errors, please send a note to errata@peachpit.com

PROJECT EDITOR	COMPOSITOR
Jim Akin	Maureen Forys, Happenstance Type-O-Rama
PRODUCTION EDITOR	INDEXER
Hilal Sala	Joy Dean Lee
COPY EDITOR	COVER DESIGN
Kathy Simpson	Andrew Shalat
	INTERIOR DESIGN
	Chris Gillespie, Happenstance Type-O-Rama

ISBN 0-321-37574-2

9 8 7 6 5 4 3 2 1

Printed and bound in the United States of America

This book is dedicated to Charissa, Dunham, and Erik.

Acknowledgements

●●●●●●●

I owe the genesis of this book to a great number of friends and family who over the years have called me for answers to a few *"quick* questions" about the Mac. The quick answers I'd give eventually crystallized into a methodology, of which readers of this book will take advantage. That said, in writing this book I would like to thank Terry Hart for his humor and marketing insights; David Leishman for his chiding and constant support; Alberto (Mr. Matorez) Inza for his friendship and encouragement; Brian Szayer for his numerous quick questions; Ann Shalat for her novice computer skills; Neal Shalat and Ed Shalat for calling on Mr. Wizard; Scott Sheppard for all of the above (well, almost all—he's no novice); Rick Newton for the writing space; Alfio Bonciani for having the first Mac I ever saw; Carlo Giorgi for finally getting one; Alan Caplin for always having one; and of course, Charissa, Dun, and Erik for everything else. Read this book, please: May it save you a phone call.

About the Author

Andrew Shalat is recognized as many things, of which writer and designer are two he can discuss publicly. His correctly spelled articles have appeared in many prestigious publications, including *Macworld,* maccentral.com, and macweek.com. His design work has popped up all over the place and continues to do so in many forms, including book covers, brochures, catalogs, CD and DVD artwork, logos, and plain old fliers. As he is a man of the people, you can even find some of work on roadsides across our fair land. Over the past 25 years he's taught literature, writing, Web design, print design, and Flash design. He's also taught his cockatoo to whistle Prokofiev. Although you may or may not find him amusing, he numbers several professionally funny people among his friends. He lives in Los Angeles with a lovely woman who claims to be his wife and, if we accept that as fact, their two sons.

Contents

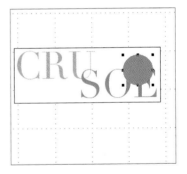

READ ME FIRST: An Introduction

●●●●●●●

Now, before we get carried away, let's get something straight. First of all, this book will not make you a designer. Take it from me, you don't want to be a designer anyway; everyone's always asking your opinion about color or where to put the piano. Forget about it—nothing but petty annoyances.

What this book will do, however, is give you enough skill and insight to make good *design decisions,* using one of the most powerful tools a designer could ever have: the Macintosh.

Solutions are the name of the game. And to arrive at solutions, we have to make design decisions.

In the real world (if designers can be said to inhabit such a place), we don't rely on software to define design work. Rather, our design decisions determine which software we use to achieve a particular design or project-oriented solution. The procedure is one of choice, more so than inspiration—resourcefulness rather than rote, process over protocol.

In a sense, all of us are designers already. We just sublimate our decisions into a habit or regular way of getting through a day. If you've ever set a table, you've touched on being a designer. You interpreted a cultural form and, either instinctively or by rote, composed a layout.

We all do our best to control, at the very least, the desktop space in front of us, placing needed materials within reach, using disparate tools for disparate uses. We are all designers, but we don't always get paid for it.

What's ironic about good design is that at its best, it's invisible. The process disappears, and the author goes unnoticed. Things *belong.* The contrast is natural; the positioning makes sense; and most of all, the intended message comes across.

Most books tell you how to use specific software packages, most of which are expensive and go through every menu item in linear fashion: A to B, B to C. That approach is sterile and noncreative. Every digital crevice and hidden user interface is brought to light, but no light of inspiration is conjured. The simple procedures (emphasis on *simple*) you'll find in this book are the driftwood and dry weeds you use to make a fire on a deserted beach.

The process you use to get something done—to finish that one particular project you've been assigned, the flier you need for the garage sale, the business card you have to have in your pocket for that three o'clock meeting today—well, you won't find that in the menu bar of Adobe Illustrator. You'll find it between the menu items. It's hiding between the software, the keyboard, and you.

So this book turns the A-to-B-to-C equation on its head. This book focuses on specific tasks. Using only the software and hardware available to you with just your Mac out of the box, we will improvise solutions and make design. The principles of good design are not limited to software packages. With just a bare-bones Macintosh and the bundled software provided therein, we *can* solve most basic design problems.

At the end of each chapter, you'll find a section called "For a Few Bucks More," where you will learn how to use Apple's iWork or other outside-the-bundle software to help solve the problems discussed in that chapter. With the insight of what you've learned, you can go beyond the intended prefabricated scope of the software.

In other words, let's use our Macs as machetes. Let's become guerilla designers. We'll use found or created graphic elements and put them together. We'll create sounds and narration and apply them to our movies ourselves. We'll take still images and make them move, literally and figuratively.

The methods you learn here will build on one another, and you'll find yourself using them in all aspects of your future production, be they simple or complex, from putting a message in a bottle to putting together a slideshow or business presentation, with or without highfalutin, expensive software.

Oh, and if anyone ever asks, put the piano in the corner of the room.

READ ME NEXT: A Basic Skill Set

There's this factory, and one morning, in the middle of the heaviest work shift, all the machinery goes down. Drills stop drilling; pumps stop pumping; confabulators stop confabulating. In a panic, the floor manager calls a repair contractor and explains the desperate situation.

After half an hour, the technician arrives. He nonchalantly walks through the factory, past the silent drills, pumps, and confabulators, to a small control box at the back of the expansive room. He opens the cabinet, peruses the switches and wiring, and removes a small screwdriver from his toolbox. He finds an inconspicuous screw and twists it a one-quarter turn. Instantaneously, the factory floor comes back to life.

The repair tech turns to the floor manager and hands him an invoice for $50,000. The floor manager says, "What's this? Fifty thousand dollars?! All you did was turn a screw."

Nonplussed, the repair tech responds, "Let me itemize it for you. The screwdriver usage fee is 25 cents. The other $49,999.75 is for knowing which screw to turn."

In design, too, knowledge and skill are far more important than fancy tools, and that's why this book focuses on making good design decisions instead of on the intricacies of the many world-class design programs available for the Macintosh. Nevertheless, every craft requires knowledge of a few basic techniques, and as we work our way through the design challenges in this book, we'll be using a very specific set of skills continually. So without further ado, here they are.

The Screen Grab

The *screen grab* is a technique for creating image files, essentially by taking a picture of some or all of whatever is in front of you on your Mac's screen. It's also the name for a file that results from that process: Performing a screen grab places a screen grab called Picture 1 on your Desktop. You may have heard these files called *screen captures* or even the more pedestrian *pictures-of-what's-on-your-Mac*. No matter what you call them, making a screen grab is an essential skill that you will be able to use in more cases than you can swing a mouse at.

The addition of Web access, a scanner, or a digital camera would increase your image options, but because we're working only with what's at hand, we won't have any artwork that we don't conjure ourselves. That makes the screen grab the Swiss army knife of out-of-the-box skills. When we have it down (and it's not that hard), we can use any of the images or patterns we put on our Desktop as elements for all types of design we produce on our Macs, from print to Web to video.

There are two types of screen grabs. The first is the *basic grab,* which takes a picture of your entire screen, from menu items and blue apple on top to your Dock on the bottom. The second is the *selection grab.* As its name implies, this method of screen grab lets you select a rectangular portion of the screen and capture it as an image.

● Use the keys highlighted above to make screen grabs.

The Basic Grab

The keyboard shortcut for the basic grab is: Shift+Command (the key with the Apple logo just to the right or left of the spacebar)+3. From here on, we'll denote key commands in this fashion: Shift+Command+3. Simple, right?

Let's try it.

Open the TextEdit application (Macintosh HD/Applications/TextEdit). The new, untitled document will have a blinking cursor, beckoning for input. Type the word **Design**. Now execute your big move: Shift+Command+3. Did you hear the camera shutter? Now look at your Desktop. You should find a new item named Picture 1.

● Here Picture 1, sitting on the Desktop.

Double-click Picture 1, and the Preview application will open to reveal an exact image of your screen at the time you took the grab.

As an aside, this form of screen grab is also a great way to get you fired from a job or at least make enemies of your co-workers. If you take a picture of the screen and then, through System Preferences, choose that picture as your Desktop pattern, it will disconcert even the most experienced Mac users. But let's save that for the sequel, *Macintosh Out of the Box Evil Tricks*.

The Selection Grab

Press the key command for the selection grab, Shift+Command+4, and your mouse pointer will become a pair of crosshairs. Place the center of the crosshairs at the corner of a rectangular region you want to capture, press and hold down the mouse button, and drag the crosshairs to the opposite corner of the rectangle (which is helpfully highlighted with a gray shadow). Release the mouse button. You will again hear the shutter click, and your selection grab will appear as a new file on your Desktop. (The Mac names all screen grabs sequentially, so the new file will be called Picture 2 if you took only one basic grab, Picture 3 if you took two, and so on.)

● Press Shift+Command+4, and then drag the crosshairs around the area you want to grab.

Now we should note that Mac OS X 10.3 and 10.4 have a few more screen-grab features we can use. One is the Grab submenu on the Services menu, which you'll find in the menu bar under the name of whichever application you happen to be using. Grab itself is also a stand-alone application hidden in the Utilities folder (Macintosh HD/Applications/Utilities/Grab). All the grab functions in the Services menu are also in the stand-alone application. The Grab application lets you take selection grabs, window grabs, and screen and timed screen grabs. The big advantage of the Grab application is that it lets you name files as you capture them and save them anywhere you like. If you're not happy using the generically named Picture 1, Picture 2 scheme, by all means grab Grab.

Using the Grab application is quick and easy (and faster still if you add it to your Dock), but if you're in a real hurry, you can access Grab from the Services menu—most of the time, that is, because functions available in the Services menu vary from application to application. Grab doesn't work in AppleWorks 6, for example, but in two other programs we'll be using (TextEdit and Pages), the Grab submenu contains three options: Screen, Selection, and Timed Screen. Screen and Selection are just like Command+Shift+3 and +4, respectively, with one important distinction: When you choose Grab from the Services menu, your image appears inside the page you're working on, at the spot where your text-insertion cursor is placed, instead of on the Desktop. This can save you several steps.

Timed Screen is an interesting feature as well; it snaps a screen grab ten seconds after you select it. That gives you time to get your mouse pointer and other extraneous clutter (such as the Services menu itself) out of the way or to switch a movie player to full-screen mode before the shutter clicks.

For the most part, however, we'll be using the global Shift+Command+3 or Shift+Command+4. That way we don't have to open a separate application unless totally necessary.

Save As PDF

One of the most versatile and unsung strengths of Mac OS X is its Save as PDF command. *PDF* stands for *Portable Document Format*, and PDF files have the useful ability to retain their appearance—including their layout and typographical features—on any computer, printer, or other device, even if (and this is a *big* "even if") the program and fonts used to create the original file aren't available. Think of it as a sort of shrink-wrap of your document, sealing in the fonts just as it seals in the flavor.

To understand this better, consider for a moment how things work without PDF: Let's say you create a beautiful flier in AppleWorks (you will, you will) and that it includes the font Apple Chancery (it won't, it won't). As you'd probably guess, Windows computers don't really know what to do with AppleWorks files, and that Apple-flavored font isn't used on many PCs, either. So if you e-mailed your flier to a Windows user, she would be unable to open or print it.

You could improve things somewhat by using AppleWorks's capability to save the file as a Windows-friendly Microsoft Word document. That would allow your friend to open and read the flier, but without the Apple Chancery font on her PC, she'd see amateurish ransom-note typography instead of your elegant design. Save the file as a PDF, however, and your poor PC-user recipient will be able to see your flier in all its intended glory—as well as print it, post it to a Web page, and so on.

When you get around to explaining the superiority of the Mac environment to your PC-using pal, be sure to mention that support for PDF is a fundamental, built-in feature of Mac OS X. What that means to us is that any document, image, or (ahem) screen grab, can be made into a PDF.

Here's how it's done:

Open the TextEdit document you used for the screen grabs; then highlight the text. We're going to do a small bit of design now. We don't have to at this stage, of course, but as long as we're making a graphic element, we may as well make it attractive.

Choose Format > Font > Show Fonts (or press the equivalent shortcut, Command-T). When the Font panel opens, apply to the highlighted text a typeface more attractive than plain old Helvetica—Papyrus, for example. Now make the size 72 point. Certainly more interesting than before, no?

● Use the Font panel to see and work with the fonts on your Mac.

Now for the PDF: Choose File > Print (or press the Command-P shortcut). In the ensuing dialog box, rather than simply choosing Print, choose Save as PDF. If you're using Mac OS X 10.3 (Panther), click the Save as PDF button; if you're using Mac OS X 10.4 (Tiger), click what looks like a PDF button but is actually a PDF pull-down menu and then choose Save as PDF. Now name your file. By default, the Mac will put it in your Documents folder; you can save it anywhere you like, but that's not really important now. What's important is that you have made a simple graphic element in PDF format through the Print dialog box.

Double-click your new PDF file. It will open in the Preview application and lead us to the next basic skill: cropping.

Cropping

Cropping is the technique of editing an image by changing its borders—isolating one element from a group, for example, or cutting out clutter around the edges. Because redefining an image's borders effectively changes its meaning, your choice of how to crop an image can be as important as selecting the subject itself.

Documentarian Ken Burns demonstrates this technique in his artful use of archival photos. By tightly focusing his camera on a specific face, he can "crop" a group photo of a jazz band or baseball team into an intimate portrait of an individual player.

Cropping an image in Preview is similar to creating a selection grab, only you don't have to twist your fingers over specific keys on the keyboard—and you don't have to get your selection right the first time. In Preview, drag your mouse over the area you want to isolate and then apply the crop by choosing Tools > Crop or by pressing Command-K. In the case of our TextEdit PDF, we can select just the word *design*, get rid of the excess space, and crop it close enough to make it a simple logotype (graphic element) that we can use later in any number of layouts and various media.

In Preview, drag your mouse around the area you want to use and then choose Tools > Crop to trim away parts of an image.

Knowing the Right Screw

So you see, when we say *basic* skills, we really mean it. Finally, there is one more set of skills that we need to mention. These skills have to do with our overall approach to design, layout, and presentation. Before we set out to put something into a medium outside our brain—such as paper, CD, film, or digital audio—we should always stop and think about our goals and our design objectives.

To guide us, we have three principles that we may as well just call Andrew's Rules of Thumb (ART™):

1. Consider our message.

2. Consider our target audience.

3. Organize and prioritize all design elements to express that message and reach that audience.

As you'll see in the chapters ahead, these principles will inform all our design decisions. They will guide our design planning, and we will invoke them often as we make our way through each stage of design execution to make sure we stay on course.

Despite the handy acronym, it's important to recognize that these rules, and the rest of this book, apply to *design* but not necessarily to *art*. It's perfectly possible to use the tools on your Mac to produce works of pure transcendent beauty, but that's not our goal here. Our focus as designers is practical: We want to get a message across to a specific audience. We'll arrange, rearrange, and rearrange again. We'll play with design elements, making *design decisions* each step of the way to convey that message effectively.

Good design always has a certain beauty, but its purpose is to serve the message, not necessarily a Higher Truth. Making an effective argument is sometimes as high a truth as we can ever want. How we stir our audience comes from a combination of all our higher senses. But we have an immediate goal first: We have to get the machines on the factory floor working. With the simple skills we've just learned, we have the basic tools to do just that.

Design depends on so many things. The tools we use affect the product we intend to make. But knowing how to use the tools we have, just as much as knowing which tools to use, gives us more choices. And choice is power. It's the difference between knowing which screw to turn and how much to turn it.

All knowledge comes at a price, of course. In this case, it will be $49,999.75, please. Or just the cost of this book. Your choice; we'll accept either.

Chapter One: Print

Here's the scenario: You've been shipwrecked on a desert island. All you have with you are your newly purchased Macintosh, a small printer, lots of paper, and enough electricity from batteries in your wreck to keep going for a few months. Unfortunately, you were planning on buying your design software at the next port of call. So you have only what came with the Mac. What are you going to do?

You have your Macintosh with you, and you're not going to just sit around waiting passively to be rescued. You're going to want to make something good out of an otherwise-dire situation. So you'll focus your energies on survival and getting rescued. Maybe, just to keep productive, you'll also start a little business venture on the side—but let's not get ahead of ourselves.

First things first: If you're ever to get yourself off this island, you'll need to get noticed. People will have to know how to find you and rescue you from your cubicle—ahem, *island.*

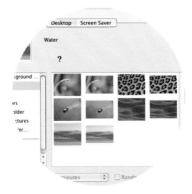
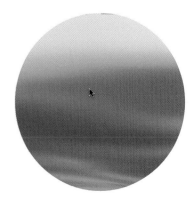

Your survival depends on getting your message out to the people you need to see it. You need to make those people aware of your situation and get them to respond the way you want them to. Come to think of it, the survival of your new business could depend on the same thing.

Nothing short of a *campaign* is in order, and it's up to you to make it work. Your resources are limited. There's an ocean of noise and confusion between you and your audience. And you've got to fashion a message and present it in a way that demands attention and gets results.

You'll need to print some fliers to stuff into bottles, along with other material to get noticed. And in case busy would-be rescuers need an extra nudge, you'll want to plan to do some follow-up communications too. Postcards should do nicely.

Survival is the name of the game. Beyond postcards, you'll want to design a logo and business card so that when you are finally rescued, you'll be able to continue the island-based enterprise you founded during your troubles. It's just like life, isn't it? You still need to be productive. You still need to make order out of the chaos, decide on priorities, and figure out which tools best help you survive and succeed. You need to make good *design decisions.*

As in life, in design there is no one "right" way of doing things, although there are many wrong ways. With that in mind, we'll try a few approaches for each project. We'll start with what we might call a primitive approach, using only a simple text editor, some graphics, and some text. Along the way, we'll uncover some basic design guidelines that will inform not just the project at hand, but also all the ensuing design problems we may face. As you might expect, after the primitive approach comes something more sophisticated, which we'll call the arranged layout. For this, we'll employ a slightly more powerful drawing application, which will gives us some versatility in layout.

Finally, we'll look at what we get if we spend a few bucks and use a prepackaged approach. Because we're trying to keep this as simple as possible—and not spend too much on anything—we'll limit our add-on software options to Apple's iWork suite. (The "suite" is really just a pair of programs: a word processor called Pages and a presentation-slideshow program called Keynote.)

For purposes of our flier, we'll limit our iWork focus to Pages, which takes a template-based approach to design that's both efficient and limited. As you work with it, you'll learn to take advantage of its efficiency, as well as when and how to push beyond its limitations.

Sometimes, all it takes to survive are a sharp rock and a good idea. Think of your Macintosh as a sharp rock. Now let's get started with the good idea.

Section 1: The Flier

⬤⬤⬤⬤⬤⬤⬤

We are going to make several fliers, so here is our first project.

The Primitive Flier

Legend says that when Michelangelo chose a piece of marble for his sculpture, he already saw the finished piece *inside* the block. All he had to do was remove the excess to reveal the form within. If we all had the vision or talent or whatever it was that Michelangelo possessed, we'd be able to look at a blank page and see as he saw: a finished design that perfectly balances words, images, and layout to convey a clear, compelling message. But odds are, we're not Michelangelos. When we look at a blank page, we have to take a different approach.

Every designer has his own way of envisioning his final piece before he actually achieves it. A lot is trial and error, or more like trial and retrial—putting things down on the page and shifting them around; making some things bigger, some smaller; aligning center or left; changing black type to gray.

Many books that purport to teach design give step-by-step instructions without leaving any room for the exploration of alternatives. This precludes an occurrence in design called the *happy accident.* Its counterpart in literature is often called *found poetry*. Imagine that you're moving the couch from one corner of the room to the other, and underneath, you discover a slip of paper that describes *chickens next to the red wheelbarrow, glazed with rainwater*. A found poem! A happy accident.

In Mac-based design, the happy accident occurs when, by some stray movement of the mouse, some extra click or an incomplete drag and drop, you discover a previously unseen design solution. There is no calculation for it, and you can't plan on it. But there is always a way to leave enough slack in the process to plan *for* it, should it occur. Let's keep that in mind as we go through any step-by-step processes here.

Our process in designing our flier may seem strict and step by step, but in actuality, we're trying to build in some room for exploration and accident. Along the way, we may want to retreat a few steps as well. Sometimes happy accidents turn sour, but even a sour design accident is a learning experience. Missteps can get you lost, and sometimes backtracking is the only escape, but sometimes those missteps reveal alternative paths, and even shortcuts, to your goal.

Speaking of which, in the case of our first project, the Primitive Flier, here's an example of what we're shooting for:

RESCUE ME

SHIPWRECKED ON A DELIGHTFULLY DESERTED ISLAND.

Please send help.
We'll be running out
of inkjet ink soon...

Not to mention sunscreen
and cool tropical drinks.

*Make a 30° turn west at Tahiti,
go straight 200 miles.*

Our final piece may or may not look exactly like the figure on page 4, but it's a *direction* in which we want to go. And the specific steps we use to get there may open other design avenues to explore.

Before we really get started on the flier, let's create a place to keep all the components we'll be assembling to create it. So let's make a new folder on the Desktop: Place the mouse pointer on the Desktop, click once to make sure the Finder is the active application, and then Control+click and choose New Folder from the pull-down menu. Type **Flier** to rename the untitled folder; then click the Desktop again to save its new name. It's a good policy to have a folder for every project you work on.

We'll be making a lot of screen grabs for the flier, and even with a project folder to put them in, things can get very confusing if we stick with the generic names the Mac gives them by default (Picture 1, Picture 2, and so on). Therefore, we'll name grab files (and all the other files we make) descriptively. To rename Picture 1, for example, just click the name below its icon. (Don't double-click; that'll open the file.) When the file's name becomes highlighted, type a new, more logical name for the file. (For reasons we'll get into later, it's a good idea to stick with a single-word name for each file. If multiple words are critical, try separating them with a dash or an underscore character—for example, two-names or two_names.)

Everyone has his own sense of order, so we won't always tell you what to name each file, and we'll generally leave it up to you to decide how to set up your project folders. If you're the type who likes to leave socks on the floor until someone else picks them up, fine, we won't nag you. It'll just be up to you to keep track of your own project files. That said, let's move forward.

This book is all about enabling you to make good creative decisions, but we need a jumping-off point for that, so you'll have to take a back seat for just a little while. Just follow the directions for a little bit, and we promise to turn you loose later.

This is basic stuff. Open TextEdit (Applications/TextEdit). In the untitled document that appears, type the words **RESCUE ME**, all caps. Highlight the text with your mouse, and set the font (Format > Font > Show Fonts) to Verdana, bold, 64 point. All type should be in black at this point. Now select just the word RESCUE, and in the Font window, change the color to a deep blue.

Before we go too much farther, let's save our work. Choose File > Save, and name the file Flier.rtf; if you want to be tidy, place it in the Flier folder on your Desktop. It's a good idea to repeat the Save command (or press its shortcut, Command + S) regularly as you work, so you won't lose changes to the file if your Mac freezes up.

When we put our flier together, the RESCUE ME headline will serve as a graphic element of our design. We'll be concerned with its role in the flier's visual composition as much as (or maybe even more than) we will be with the words as text. So we'll turn the words into a graphic element by taking a picture of them. Press the Return key a few times to get the blinking cursor out of the way, and use a selective screen grab (Command+ Option+4) to isolate the headline.

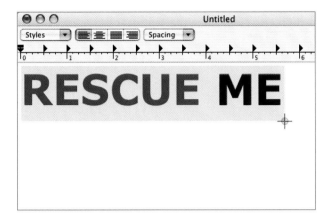

Now we can insert that graphic into the page. Rename the grab file, if you like, and drag it from the Desktop to the TextEdit page; it'll be inserted at the spot on the page where the blinking cursor is located. Please don't get confused here: You've got headline text, followed by a graphic that duplicates that text. To the eye, the headlines are indistinguishable, but the way each version behaves on the page is very different: Place your mouse pointer over one headline and click. Now do the same with the other.

When you click the type-based headline, your pointer becomes a text-insertion point; you can select and edit or resize the text, and if you type additional characters, the headline will flow. Type enough characters ahead of the headline, and ME will get pushed along until it wraps onto a new line of text, separated from RESCUE. When you click the graphic, the whole headline is selected as a unit, with resize handles around its perimeter; you can't change the text, but if you drag the headline anywhere on the page, and even stick it in between text characters, the relative positions of RESCUE and ME will never change.

Play around a bit to get a feel for the difference between the text and graphic versions of the headline; then delete the text version to avoid confusion. The RESCUE ME graphic is all we need. We don't need to edit it anymore.

More important for the purposes of our flier, the headline will serve primarily as a graphic element in our design. Its visual appearance, including the relative size and positioning of the words it contains, will be as important to our layout as the meaning of those words (and maybe even more important).

Formatting the headline as a graphic will help you start learning, here and now, to see how elements on a page, including text, work together in a purely visual sense.

To understand this idea better, try an experiment: Grab a magazine ad and squint at it, so that your eyes go out of focus for a moment. Rather than seeing the content of the ad, look at the structure and relationship of the elements of the layout. (An alternative that's more ambitious but less Clint Eastwood is to study ads published in a language that's unfamiliar to you.) The point isn't that content is unimportant. But our main concern with page layout is the act of *seeing* the page, not reading or interpreting it.

The advantages of formatting our headline as a graphic are practical as well as functional; they have to do with the reusability. If we decide to use a headline or other text-based element in documents or designs other than the flier, saving it as a graphic sort of freezes the object in a preferred state. It makes it more versatile and useful to us in the long run. This approach sometimes takes the form of an after-the-fact design decision. A successful one-shot project, for example, might spawn follow-up designs that use elements of the original. In such cases, it's handier to use prebuilt design elements than to re-create them for each new project. Even with elements that are purely type-based, such as slogans, taglines, and simple logos, converting to graphics is often smarter as well, because it prevents design inconsistencies that can result from different applications' type-handling quirks.

Now let's add some more text to our flier. We *could* type anything at all, but if we're going to think like designers, we should step back and ask what our audience will find compelling. To guide us, let's recall Andrew's Rules of Thumb (ART™):

1. Consider our message.

2. Consider our target audience.

3. Organize and prioritize all design elements to express that message and reach that audience.

Now that we have some rules of thumb, let's do some strategizing. Here's a thought process we might want to consider:

We want to make our audience *really* want to come rescue us, right? And what messages might accomplish that? Well, we could make our predicament seem incredibly dire so that they'll rush to the rescue out of pity, compassion, and humanity. But let's be real; we're really narrowing our target market if we're going to count on a random compassionate person to find our message in a bottle.

Not only that, emphasizing our dire straits makes the message all about *us*, and our campaign (*any* campaign) will have better odds of success if it focuses on the audience and what's in it for *them*. So let's opt for the positive and describe how much fun it'll be to come to our aid:

> *SHIPWRECKED ON A DELIGHTFULLY DESERTED ISLAND.*
>
> *Please send help. We'll be running out of inkjet ink soon…*
>
> *Not to mention sunscreen and cool tropical drinks.*
>
> *Make a 30° turn west at Tahiti, go straight 200 miles.*

As the song says, we're accentuating the positive. It's important to take a stance, set a tone, and follow through. This is true of every aspect of design, marketing, and advertising. In literature and art, it's called *voice*. In film, it's called *point of view*. On the Web, it's both, because the Web encompasses both disciplines.

Having established our voice, let's focus on making the flier interesting. We need to collect our graphic elements. Where shall we find them, all alone on the beach, with naught but our trusty Macintosh, you ask? Right under our noses, dear friend, right under our noses.

Open System Preferences (located either in your Dock or in the Apple menu on at the far-left end of the menu bar). Inside System Preferences, select Desktop & Screen Saver.

Click the Screen Saver button, select Beach from the list that appears, and watch the preview window fill with scenes of sea and sand. Let the screen-saver preview run through a few times so that you get a good sense of all the images that you have at your fingertips. Now for the fun part: Let's snag some of these enticing images with the selection screen grab tool. Press Command+Option+4 to get the selection tool; click the top-left corner of the preview window; and, keeping the mouse button pressed down, drag the pointer to the lower-right corner of the window. (This can be a hit-or-miss exercise.) When the preview window contains an image you like, release the mouse button to capture it. Do this several times. Our project requires only two images, but it's good to give yourself several options to choose among.

Now we have some images to tantalize our target audience. Quit System Preferences.

Look on the Desktop for the icon of the last screen grab you made (the one with the largest number after *Picture* in its name). Rename it something memorable (Beach1 works). Click the icon, drag it onto the TextEdit page, and release your mouse button.

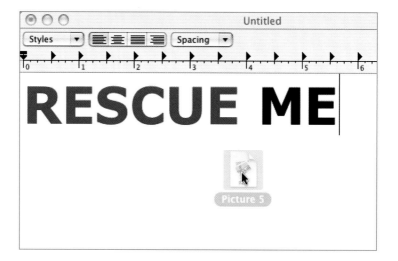

Repeat these steps with all your Beach-image screen grabs. Depending on where your cursor was as you dragged the images onto the page, the images will be stacked up in a heap among the text and headline. Don't worry about that right now.

Pick your two favorite images; then click each of the others in turn and press the Delete key to get rid of them. When only the keepers remain, drag them so that they are arranged side by side below the text, like we've done in the figure on page 11.

Now that we have all the elements on the page, we can finally start arranging (*read*: designing) the flier.

Here's a little philosophy for you: Think of a page layout as a conversation. The elements on the page (graphics, text, and headlines) all "talk" to one another and, ultimately, to the audience. An effective design draws the viewer in and lets each design element speak to him in turn.

If a page is a conversation, and the goal of its design is to bring the audience into the conversation, let's push our metaphor a little harder and consider the universal human habit of eavesdropping. (Don't worry—we'll get back to design before long.)

Despite its shady reputation, eavesdropping isn't just fun—it's also natural. We all do it, even when we don't want to; we can't help ourselves. Take a few minutes sometime (when you're back in civilization) to go to a public space—a park or restaurant, the more noisy and crowded, the better—and sit near other people. Before long, even if everyone's blabbing at once, even if you're doing your best to resist, your ears will filter out the crowd and zero in on a conversation nearby. It's nothing to be embarrassed about; human nature makes it more or less inevitable.

Less predictable, however, is which of the many conversations around you will attract your radar. That couple's political debate? The stock tips those ladies are swapping? The joke the busboy is telling the waitress? Your largely unconscious choice depends mostly on you, the audience: who you are (your age, career, and interests), your mood, what's on your mind, and so on. More than anything else, those personal attributes determine which conversation will intrigue you most.

We Mac users are naturally curious, with broad interests, so it's not hard to imagine a crowd in which at least a couple of conversations have the potential to hook you. Under those circumstances, the delivery of a conversation starts to influence your radar. A few choice words that pop out of one discussion might pull you in. A speaker's confident voice or infectious laugh might swing you to another. Your ears might even take cues from your other senses, steering your selection to a speaker with alluring cologne, a sharp Italian suit, or killer tattoos.

It follows from this that someone with a clear understanding of your needs, interests, and moods could concoct a conversation you'd find interesting. They could even hire actors you'd be likely to find appealing (or trustworthy or amusing) and have them enact it at your favorite hangout, in hopes of triggering the radar that turns you from eavesdropper to listener. (That might seem like a crazy idea, but it's what advertisers try to do at TV "hangouts" all the time.)

The connection between eavesdropping and design (this book is about design, remember?) is in Andrew's Rules of Thumb, at the junction of Rule 1, "Consider our message," and Rule 2, "Consider our target audience." A good design contains a message that's relevant to its target audience, presented in a visual "conversation" calculated to convert that audience from eavesdropping to paying attention just long enough to convey its message.

The content of the elements determines the topic of the conversation, and the elements' arrangement on the page—the design—sets the conversation's pace and tone. The design cues the audience instantly, for example, as to whether a page is meant to amuse, inform, warn, or entice; whether its message is brief or complex; and which ideas (in the form of words or images) pop out to entice an eavesdropper. The design provides an entry point where the audience should jump in and a flow that leads from one element to the next.

So, getting back to our flier, how do we want our conversation to sound? Because we're working on the cheap here, so to speak, we'll make some very basic decisions, keeping the message clear, and giving the images and text relatively equal prominence. We have to consider the context of the message and its relationship to the target reader.

Each element of our flier should be distinct from but consistent with the others, because each has a different but interlocking function in the flier's design. You may have heard that other rule of thumb that you shouldn't use more than three different fonts on the same page. Although this is not always true, keeping it simple is a good idea. *Simple* and *effective* should be our watchwords.

Of the elements on the page, their prominence or obscurity, eminence or unimportance, depend on several factors—not just size, but also *color*, *shape*, *proximity* to other elements, and *style* (especially in the case of type). So when we first set up the page elements, we'll do so in a neutral fashion. Then, when the elements are on the page, knowing what we want to say and taking in our considerations and rules of thumb, we make design decisions about how the elements will relate to one another— which will lead the conversation, speak loudest, and so on.

Let's take a look at the content of this flier. We can categorize our text as:

- A *headline* (RESCUE ME), which speaks first and loudest, with the words most likely to pop out of our message

- A *subhead* (SHIPWRECKED ON A DELIGHTFULLY DESERTED ISLAND), designed to hook audience member s by using our strategy of appealing to their desire for luxury and relaxation

- A *call to action* (Please send help. We'll be running out of inkjet ink soon…)

- A *tagline* (Not to mention sunscreen and cool tropical drinks) that uses humor to nudge the audience toward our objective

- *Specific directions* (Make a 30° turn west at Tahiti, go straight 200 miles) that enable the audience to follow through on that action.

Note the degree symbol in the directions text. Easy stuff. Find that symbol by pressing Option+0 (zero).

TIP: IF YOU HAVE SOME FREE TIME—AND BEING STRANDED ON AN ISLAND, THAT'S PRETTY MUCH A GIVEN, ISN'T IT?—CHECK OUT THE SPECIAL CHARACTERS MENU ITEM IN TEXTEDIT (EDIT > SPECIAL CHARACTERS). YOU'LL FIND ALTERNATIVE CHARACTERS, DINGBATS, AND OTHER ODD TYPE OPTIONS THAT YOU MAY WANT TO USE SOMETIME IN THE FUTURE. NOW BACK TO OUR FLIER, ALREADY IN PROGRESS.

Now that we've got all our players on the stage, let's get our conversation going. First, we'll do some arranging for a little more flair. In our primitive, or simple, flier methodology, we can't really do much with the images other than put them in complementary and effective positions on the page. Part of the reason we call this a primitive methodology has to do with the limitations of the software we're using. TextEdit wasn't designed for page layout; it's a text editor. But its simplicity is also a benefit at this stage. Our choices are limited, and sometimes limited choices free us to concentrate on other aspects of our design. This refers directly to a corollary to Andrew's Rules of Thumb, the Lemonade Principle:

- Make negatives into positives. When options are limited by technology (or budget, deadline, and so on), get creative, and you can still do good design.

- Got lemons? Make lemonade.

Manipulate the positioning of the images on the page by click+dragging them to any cursor point on the page.

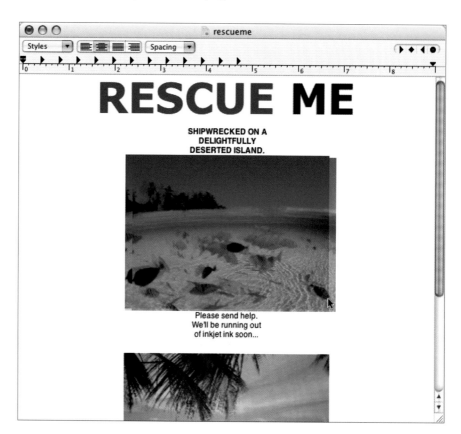

Our headline is actually a graphic (remember, we took that grab right from our text), and we'll position it at the top of the page. Drag the two-color RESCUE ME graphic to the top.

After you've placed the subhead directly below RESCUE ME, adjust the subhead typeface to make it a little more prominent.

We already know how to change type and typestyle in this application. To wit: Format > Font > Show Fonts (or press the Command+ T shortcut). From the Font palette, we can specify font family, style, size, and color.

As with the headline, we'll style the subhead in boldface and *all caps* (all letters capitalized), to convey urgency. When we choose the typeface, we'll look for a style that communicates the urgency of our situation but also lets our subhead stand independent from the headline without antagonizing it.

Making the subhead smaller than the main headline will help set it apart, but to further reinforce its independence, we'll employ another design technique—the use of serif and sans-serif fonts to offset each other. *Serifs* are little bits of ornamentation that appear on the tips of letters in some typefaces (including the one used to set this paragraph). The little crossbars at the top and bottom of a capital *I* are serifs, for example.

Serifs are an all-or-nothing deal in type design; a font either has them or it doesn't. Those that do are called serif fonts; those that don't are called *sans-serif*.

Because RESCUE ME is in a sans-serif font (Verdana), we'll use a serif font for the subhead. Take some time to explore the different typefaces available in Fonts palette. If you're using Mac OS 10.3 or 10.4, you might want to open the Font Book program in your Applications folder; it lets you browse your fonts, view full-alphabet samples of them, and even group them in collections that become available from the Font palette. If you're feeling really ambitious, you can create Serif and Sans-Serif collections, and drag each font into the appropriate collection as you view it. It'll take a little while, but it'll make font-choosing simpler in the future.

As you peruse the fonts, remember that we don't want our subhead to shout louder than the headline. Don't get carried away. Fliers are serious business. (That's what I once heard a graphic designer say. "Fliers," he said. "They're serious business." Last I heard, he sells real estate now. And come to think of it, fliers *are* important in real estate. Well, I guess he was right.)

When the subhead typeface is set, click+drag either of your Beach screen-saver grabs, and place it directly below the subhead.

Click+drag the other Beach screen-saver grab, and place it below the call-to-action text. The tagline and directions should be situated at the bottom of the page.

Now it's time to stylize the text. We'll aim for a first-person, intimate yet serious tone. Select the call-to-action text, and choose American Typewriter, regular, 18 point. There's something urgent yet personal about a typewritten letter, which makes sense here.

It may help if you experiment with some other typefaces as well. Open a new document, and type the call-to-action text; then copy and paste it five or six times. For each line, assign a different typeface, with varied sizes. You may want to write the name of each typeface you've assigned *in that face*. This page can act as a quick reference that shows the relative effectiveness of various fonts face to face, as it were. It can also become a handy guide for you in the future.

Now apply the same face and style to the tagline text. Finally, select the directions text, but instead of using the same font, refer back to our headline font and use Verdana, bold italic, 12 point. (See the original illustration for line breaks in the text.)

We're still not finished. If, as we discussed earlier, layout is like a conversation, we must respect one of the most important, yet overlooked, aspects of successful discourse: the pause. Pauses help regulate the speed and the rhythm of your message. Even on a page like this, in which the entire contents can be grasped in a couple of seconds, a pause allows one idea to sink in before another builds on it. In layout terms, we effect pauses with spacing, with changes in type size or style, or with graphic elements. In this case, we'll use the most basic of all graphic elements: the line.

First, select everything (Edit > Select All); then click the center alignment icon just above the ruler in your TextEdit document window. Now, back near the top of the page, just between the headline and the subhead, type a horizontal line, _____, that extends just beyond the length of the headline.

Makes a difference, no?

Near the bottom of the page, insert your cursor at the beginning of the directions text. Press Return. Now move your cursor back up to the line you just vacated. Type another horizontal line just beyond the edges of the image above. This line should take on the same style as the directions text (Verdana bold italic). You can also copy and paste the rule line to save some time.

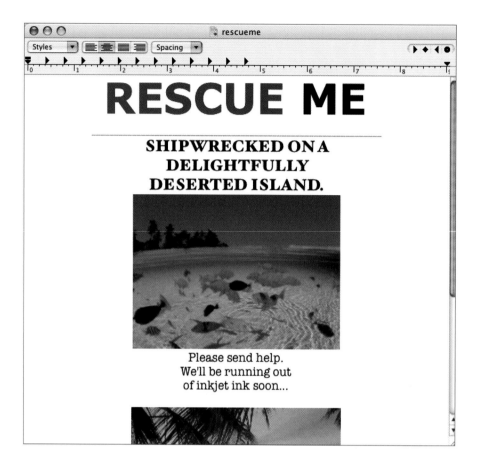

There you have it. Print your primitive flier.

Suitable for framing? Not quite. In fact, depending on the type of printer you have, you may notice that the lush photos we placed in the flier look… well, less than lush when you print them out.

The reason has to do with the technical issue of image resolution. A full discussion of this topic could fill another book, but in a nutshell, *resolution* refers to the density of tiny dots arranged, like tiles in a mosaic, to reproduce images on printed pages or your Mac's screen. Although there are printing methods that get around this problem, breaking up images into what seems like random specks (look up the term *stochastic* when you get back to civilization), for the most part, your printer will want higher-density images rather than lower-density ones.

Printing requires greater dot density (higher resolution) than displaying an image onscreen. When you view an image designed for print (such as a picture from a digital camera) onscreen at actual size, your Mac automatically scales down the original image to match the resolution of your screen, in effect creating a lookalike mosaic from fewer tiles. When you print an image designed for display onscreen (like most Web images and our screen-saver grabs), the Mac must attempt to do the reverse—deciding from a relatively small number of tiles how to fill a larger mosaic grid.

The results are typically less than spectacular, but they're good enough for desert-island work. So roll up your flier, put it in that empty beer bottle, and send it off to the rescue.

The Arranged-Layout Flier

TextEdit allows us to do only very basic layout, mostly vertical. Although this arrangement has the benefit of simplicity, it doesn't always help us drive home our message as effectively as we might like. Bundled with your new Mac, however, is a more powerful program that will help your design evolve a bit further. We'll use that program, AppleWorks, to recombine the elements of our primitive flier in a more sophisticated design that conveys our message more effectively, or at the very least, differently, taking advantage of certain aspects of layout that we couldn't achieve in TextEdit.

In AppleWorks, freed from the vertical layout TextEdit forces on us, we can change the rhythm of the flier in different ways. Placing images shoulder to shoulder with text, for example, allows words and pictures to converse in complex ways without necessarily making the viewer pause (as in the primitive flier). By giving us greater freedom to control the proximity and alignment of text and images, AppleWorks gives our designs greater freedom to guide the reader's eye, to clarify and reinforce our flier's message.

All this does add a bit of weight to our design decisions. We actually have to think harder about what we're doing. We can't sit back and let our program's limitations make design choices for us (or blame them for bad design decisions). There's more at stake. We must be even more creative. Egads. Take a deep breath, and get ready to fire up AppleWorks.

If you were ever a fan of the Little Engine That Could, you can appreciate the often-overlooked AppleWorks. Think of it as a stalwart tool that mostly can.

AppleWorks combines word processing, drawing, painting, presentation, spreadsheet, and database modules in an easy, user-friendly, and somewhat simplistic interface. Leave the spreadsheet and database for the ship's accountants; we'll concentrate on the drawing module.

Find AppleWorks in your Applications folder, and open it by double-clicking its icon. At first blush, you're presented a choice what type of application you want to use. Please choose Drawing.

As you might expect in a jack-of-all-trades program, AppleWorks's drawing module isn't as powerful as other dedicated illustration applications, but it's vastly more powerful than TextEdit. For our needs, it's fine, but it does have a very significant limitation you need to be aware of: Unlike most Mac OS X applications, the aging AppleWorks program lacks the ability to remember and undo multiple actions. It can only ever Undo the last thing you did, so be careful.

Choose Format > Rulers > Show Rulers. Notice that the white workspace measures about 8″ across. Because a standard letter-size sheet in the United States is 8.5″ x 11″, this must mean something. What the Drawing application has done is show you only the printable portion of the page; the margins, which cannot be printed on, are hidden. When making design choices, we want to consider the entire page, so choose Window > Page View. Now you should see a 0.25″ margin to the left and the right of your ruler.

By now you're probably itching to get designing (and rescued), but be patient. Understanding our design program's setup and rulers is anything but a waste of time. Going back and forth from one working view to another is a large part of designing on the Mac. If you recall, earlier in this chapter, we squinted to blur our vision so we could see a page as just elements. In the same way, when we work in an application, using rulers and guides and all the other mundane but technically important features can distract our eyes. Until you get to the point where those gridlines and ruler hash marks become invisible to your creative eye, it's important to know how to turn them on and off, so you can see the effects of your changes and envision what the final piece will look like before you're finished. It's the way architects and builders can look beyond the scaffolding on a construction site and envision the edifice to come.

Now that we've got the measure of our workspace, let's place our design elements there. Choose File > Insert, which will present a navigation dialog box. AppleWorks is oddly persnickety about insertions. In the bottom-left corner of the dialog box is a File Format pull-down menu. By default, this menu wants you to find only AppleWorks files. Because we have none (neither are we looking for any), let's change that to All Available. Now the graphic world in our computer opens up to us like a lotus in bloom. (Sorry about that. Doing graphic design makes me wax poetic at times.)

Go to your Desktop, and if you haven't cleaned up from the last exercise, you should still have a few screen grabs lying around. Scroll through the generically named Pictures, and find the RESCUE ME graphic.

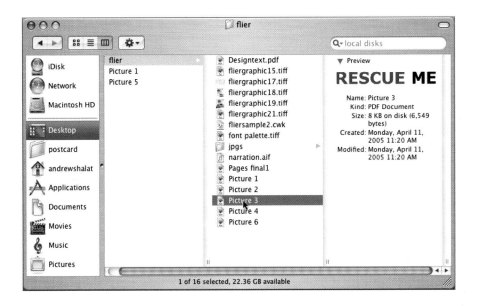

Insert the grab. Now the graphic will appear in the center of your page, only this time with eight anchor points around its perimeter. Click+dragging one of those points will let you resize the image. Be careful, though—by click+dragging one of the points, you can distort your image. Unfortunately, unlike other drawing applications that let you constrain your image scaling by holding down the Shift key while resizing, AppleWorks has no such facility. So for the time being, we won't scale the RESCUE ME headline. Instead, we'll move it toward the top of the page. Put the arrow cursor within the perimeter of the graphic, and simply click+drag the graphic into position.

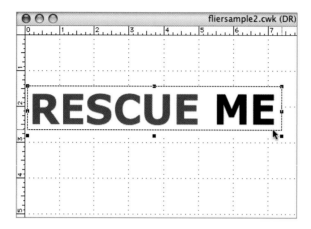

Now get the other two Beach screen grabs, and insert each into the page. You'll notice that in this exercise, we're inserting graphics first and text later. Makes you think, doesn't it?

If you click+drag the last graphic you added to the workspace, you'll notice that you can use it to cover other objects. In fact, AppleWorks stacks each object in its own invisible layer; you can shuffle objects up and down in the stack by using the Move Forward and Move Backward commands in the Arrange menu.

Click one of your beach graphics, and resize it to about 75% by choosing Arrange > Scale by Percent. Position the image to the left side, nestled below the RESCUE ME headline.

Now select RESCUE ME, and again choosing Arrange > Scale by Percent, resize it so that it begins at the 0.5″ mark and ends at the 7.5″ mark of your page ruler. The scaling percentage is about 125, but getting it right may take a few tries.

You may be tempted just to grab some anchor points and stretch the headline to fit, but don't do it; distorting type, even just a little bit, compromises the integrity of its font.

Soapbox alert: As a note to any aspiring layout mavens, typography is a very genteel art, and we should respect the scale and proportions of type-face design. Distortion rarely does much to enhance the beauty of a well-designed font and in most cases works against the type's embedded aesthetic.

Using the toolbar on the left side of your screen, select the Text tool. Using the Text tool, click+drag a square area to the right of the resized Beach graphic, about the same size as that graphic.

At this point, we have two choices: We can retype our original text, or we can open the previous flier, copy that text, and paste it in here. Pasting the previous text will save you the steps involved in stylizing the text. The choice is yours.

If you choose to retype, you'll have to restyle the text. Choose Text > Font. The complete list of the fonts installed on your system will open. Find your preferred typeface, and select it with a mouse click.

If you've copied and pasted the text from the earlier flier, you'll want to break it into separate text frames. This may be as tedious as simply typing in the first place, but no one ever said there would be any free rides in design, right? The most efficient way to get this done is to select your text from the bottom up, up to but not including the subhead. Then cut it (press Command+X). Next, you'll have to reselect the Type tool (because with each click, your tool returns to the default arrow pointer). Drag out a new text area, and paste. Repeat this process until each section of your text (subhead, call to action, tagline, and directions) has its own separate block.

As you can see, a drawing application handles text very differently from a word processor. Double-clicking a text object selects the text inside the block, so you can edit, change or resize fonts, and so on. Clicking a text object once selects it as a block, with anchor points similar to those we've seen on image objects. Click and drag inside the selected block to move it around, or click and drag an anchor point to resize the block. As a test, click a text block once and drag its bottom corner anchor. Make the box tall and thin, short and wide, and so on, and see how the text wraps to fit inside the box. Other than the *hard returns* you create by pressing Return, line breaks in text boxes are dictated by the positions of text-block anchors.

Restore your text box to normal, and position the subhead (SHIP-WRECKED…) to the right of the first Beach image. Make sure to resize the text block so that it doesn't go farther right than the RESCUE ME headline graphic.

Select the tagline (Not to mention…), and remove the hard return between the words *sunscreen* and *and.* Stretch the tagline across the page, from 0.5″ to 7.5″. Keep its left alignment.

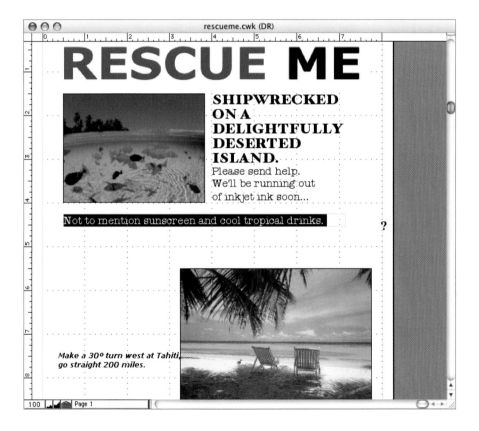

Let's take a look at the whole page now and get a sense of its layout. In the bottom-left corner of the active window is the scaling percentage. If you don't have that large a monitor, you may be seeing only part of your page. Click the scale number, and choose a percentage that allows you to see the complete page. For a 15˝ monitor, for example, you'll need to choose 75%.

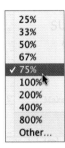

The subhead font and text size work well with our headline, but our message will be more balanced and coherent if we create a visual link between the first image of our "delightfully deserted island" and its description in the subhead to its right. Aligning the top and bottom lines of the subhead text with the top and bottom of the image will make the reader's eye take in the image and the text as a unit; the relationship between words and image will be confirmed.

To do this without disturbing our nicely balanced font sizes, we'll increase the leading of the subhead. *Leading* (rhymes with *heading*) is the space between lines of type, measured upward from the baseline of your type, usually in *points.* (There are 72 points in an inch.) Our subhead is in 24-point type; when that text is single-spaced, the leading is typically about 16 points. We'll increase that to about 34 points to air out the text block and align it with the image.

To do that, choose Format > Paragraph. Change the measurement units in the Line Spacing field from lines (li) to points (pt), type **34**, and click Apply. If the text doesn't align quite right with the image, experiment with different line-spacing values. You can click Apply each time to test the results without using up an Undo.

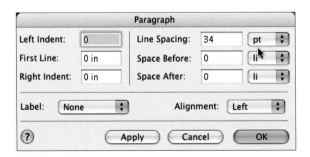

Pull the second Beach image down and to the right, settling the bottom-right corner of the image at 7.75˝ across and 9.5˝ down. The middle space on the page opens to us.

Let's change the typeface of the call to action and the tagline. Select the call to action with the arrow tool; double-click inside it to activate the Text tool. Remove line breaks, and triple-click to select all the text. Choose Text > Font, and select Comic Sans MS. Now choose Text > Style > UPPERCASE.

Do the same with the tagline text block. Now move the tagline down to the left of the Beach image near the bottom of the page.

Run the call-to-action line laterally across the whole page, but move its left margin in two taps of your cursor. Increase the size of the text (Text > Size > 36 point). The text will fill out the space in the middle of the page. While we're at it, let's move the errant directions text to the bottom of the page.

Select the tagline, using the Text tool, and resize the type to 24 point (Text > Size > 24 point). Now align the text to the right (Format > Paragraph).

Finally, using the Text tool, select the directions text. Change the type to American Typewriter, 18 point, and center-align it.

We still have some work to do on this. But let's look at what we've wrought thus far. We still have a strong headline. The subhead is reinforced by and unified with the first image but nevertheless has become less prominent. The call to action has become the focal point of the whole piece, by virtue of its position and relative size on the page.

Select the last words of the call to action (*ink soon…*), and change their color to a medium gray. Use the Text Color formatting button in the bottom-left corner of the toolbar palette. Choose the text, select the *T* icon. and click the small color grid just to the right and up in the toolbar palette. Now choose a color. This will emphasize the desperation and impending doom we're facing, running low on ink.

Select the Rectangle tool in the toolbar palette. Starting at the left margin, begin drawing a rectangle from the top of the upper Beach image to the bottom of the lower Beach image, filling from left margin to right. The rectangle will obscure everything on your page except the headline and the directions. With the rectangle still selected, click the Fill formatting icon (two icons above the *T* icon in the toolbar palette). Now click the color grid, and select a sandy shade of tan.

Choose Arrange > Move to Back.

Now select the left anchor, and resize the rectangle to align with the left edge of the top Beach image. Do the reverse on the right, aligning it with the right edge of the bottom Beach image. Make sure that the rectangle has no line. To do this, select the Pen formatting tool, click the Line Weight button, and choose None.

This island of color lets the images and text rest a bit and gives the eye a comfortable place to take in our message. More than that, our choice of a sand-colored background reflects the ideas of *beach* and *island.*

Let's look at the flier in terms of the conversation metaphor. What's the tone of this piece? Does it invite eavesdropping? In comparison with the earlier primitive flier, the breakup of the space makes for a more interesting discourse among the elements. The layout should take your eye on a designed and intentional path, shaped something like a letter *Z,* starting from the top with the RESCUE ME headline, down to the left to rest on the first Beach image, across and back to the left, across to the other Beach image, and finally resting on the directions across the bottom. Although the tone is declarative and insistent, it's also relaxed and inviting.

The colors don't shout, but the combination of blues, tan, and grays soothes the tone of the piece. The zigzag movement of the piece makes for more interesting reading, both visually and intellectually. Along with the subtle use of colors that relate to the meaning and structure of the piece (sand, sea, sky), your message is carried across several layers. Good job.

For a Few Bucks More

One day, an outrigger from a neighboring island rows up to the beach. Our friendly visitor carries with him various fruits, berries, and cloth, as well as a sealed box of new software. Lo, it's Apple's iWork suite, which consists of two programs that can help us in our design efforts: an updated version of Keynote, Apple's program for creating presentation slideshows; and Pages, which is billed as a word processor but features some powerful page-layout tools.

Nothing in this life comes for free. We trade a few coconuts for the fruit and berries, but the islander wants 79 clams (which we've worked hard to catch, mind you) for the iWork. He mumbles something in his language that we take to mean "The box fell off the back of a passing plane, and I'm not making a profit." It's not as though we haven't heard that one before. At least there's no tax.

Install iWork, and open Pages. This page-layout program comes with pre-designed, clean, clear templates. Don't be dismayed; we can still improvise in our own ways, using the preformatted themes Apple has provided us. We can gain ownership of our work.

Upon opening Pages, you will be asked to choose a template. On the left side of the window are rubrics of what kinds of documents you have available. On the right are previews of all of those templates.

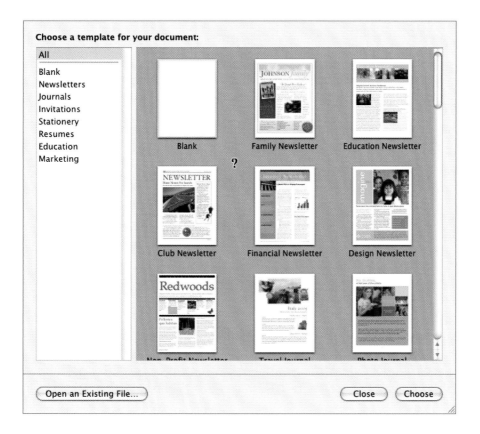

The most difficult part of designing a flier in Pages is deciding which template best fits your needs. In a sense, it's a focused design decision, which means we have to revert to Andrew's Rules of Thumb once again—in this case, the first two. Let's remind ourselves:

1. Consider our message.

2. Consider our target audience.

I repeat these rules not because we must change our expectations, but because we must compare them with what Pages has to offer. The template designs that Pages proffers out of the box may not always be an exact fit, but they are in most cases close enough for a good starting point.

Creating layouts in Pages is extremely easy. In this exercise, we'll create two fliers, using the same information and content as before. This way, we can compare the different effect two different layout designs can achieve while keeping the same content.

All the templates or themes included in Pages are well balanced and uniformly stylized. The designs come equipped with text styles (which we'll see in a minute), *text wraps* (buffer areas around images that prevent text from overlapping images), and coordinated color schemes. If nothing else, the templates Pages provides are excellent examples of simple but effective layout.

Pages templates are nice starting points, but we shouldn't let their prescribed uses (School Report, Photo Journal, Family Newsletter, and so on) limit our intentions. So when we choose a theme, we might want to try to ignore the intended use and look at the themes in terms of layout—how the images and text relate to one another on the page. Remember, we can change all the elements the program provides us. We just want to consider which layouts might best suit our very simple needs. We're not making a newsletter—just a flier.

So let's get back to choosing a template. For our first Pages flier, choose the Design Newsletter. Why? It has a strong and yet simple design, dominated by a headline–image pair that has a good chance of catching a viewer's eye and drawing him in as a reader. The basic juxtaposition of image and text guide the eye through a reading flow similar to that of our AppleWorks flier, and the design suits our need for interest, urgency, and readability.

Before we adapt this design to our purposes, let's once again familiarize ourselves with our software tools. Pages and Keynote share a simple user-friendly interface, mixing icons with clear labels and interactive tools. It doesn't take long to figure out how most of the tools work.

Most of the tools you'll be using in Pages are in the toolbar along the top of the main Pages window. The toolbar shows both icons and names, and you can think of them as icon-based menu items. If you rest your mouse pointer over any of the icons for a moment, a small note appears, explaining the use of each tool.

One of the most important tools, which we'll be using quite a bit, is the Inspector. Clicking this tool brings up a small palette with its own icon toolbar at the top. Each tool within the Inspector is specific to one of the objects or tools from the original toolbar. So if you choose an image on the page and then click the Graphic icon in the Inspector, you get to change, add, and transform that image. The same goes for type, layout, position of objects, rotation, and other commands. As we go through this exercise, we'll use most of the tools from the main toolbar and then tweak and transform them with the Inspector.

After we open our new Pages layout, a window appears, displaying the prefab template. Notice that there are no grids or rulers—just clean, well-designed, and well-balanced layout, populated with faux-Latin content.

All the content in Pages templates can be replaced with our own content. Before we get started on that, choose File > Save (or press the Command+ S shortcut) to save the new file, and change its name from Untitled to something more fitting, such as pages_flier.

Choose View > Show Rulers. Even though everything has been pre-designed, you should always have an objective sense of measurement.

Next, choose View > Show Layout. Now you can see the outlines of each object on the page. These guides help you when you're manipulating and rearranging page elements. The gray outlines also show you where empty or (up to this point) unused image or text areas lie.

Using the Design Newsletter template, we'll replace the images there with our earlier screen grabs. (Remember when you made that RESCUE ME headline text into a graphic? Now you see how versatile it is to have as a graphic image rather than fluid text.)

There is a green block on the left, with the word *imagine*. Double-click *imagine*. The text appears as selected *and* horizontal. Replace it with the word, all caps, *HELP*.

To the right of HELP are two lines of Latin: EUISMOD ELEMENTUM. Double-click, and change that text to STRANDED AND NEED TO BE RESCUED.

Now click the photo of the children on the right. If you hold your mouse over the selected image, an instructional yellow band will tell you, "This image is a placeholder. Drag a new image here to replace it." But where do you have a replacement image? Why, from our Beach screen-saver grabs, of course. (When you get back to civilization, you'll be able to use any images you can collect from your digital camera or draw in any illustration or digital-imaging application.)

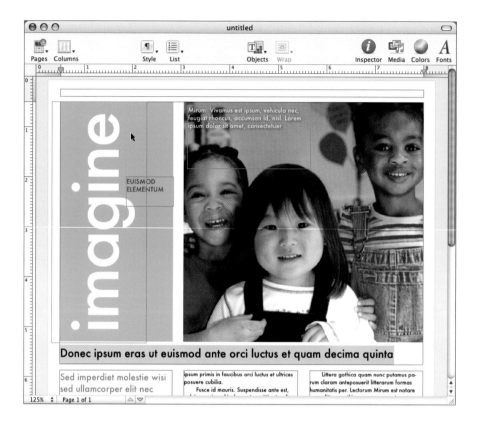

We can either open a Finder window and locate our grab or choose Insert > Choose to locate and select our image. Using either method, please find one of your Beach screen-saver grabs, and place it on the Design Newsletter page.

Notice that the image is not necessarily the same size as the placeholder that preceded it. But choosing the image with a click gives you anchor points that allow you to resize or move the object.

Move the image so that it aligns with the top edge of the green field behind HELP. Pages can help align objects as well. Choose Pages > Preferences, the and click the Show Guides at Object Edges option. Now when the edge of an object you're moving aligns with the edge of any other object on the page, a guide line will appear to let you know the objects are lined up.

Let's remove the faux-Latin text that sits on top of the image by clicking it and pressing the Delete key on the keyboard.

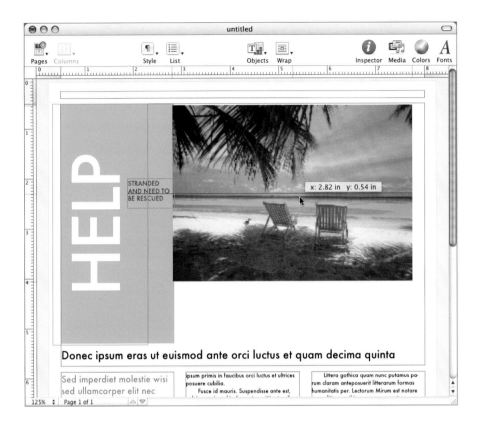

In the white space below the image, insert the RESCUE ME graphic (Insert > Choose).

Similar to AppleWorks, Pages lets us zoom out by choosing the percentage located in the bottom-left corner of the window. Choose Fit Page if you're using a smaller screen or 100% if you have an oversize monitor, just so long as you can see the whole page.

You may want to toggle from Layout view to Preview (View > Show/Hide Layout) to get a sense of how your page will look when printed.

This layout is not really the same as the flier at all, is it? There's a lot more text. We don't have to use it, of course, and in this case, we'll want to replace this placeholder text with our own story. It's important to use something other than the faux Latin, even if it's a repeating bit of nonsense, as long as you supplant the existing text.

NOTE: THERE IS A TECHNICAL REASON FOR THIS THAT INVOLVES THE WAY APPLE HAS FORMATTED THE PLACEHOLDER TEXT. UNFORTUNATELY, PAGES WON'T LET YOU SELECT ONLY ONE PARAGRAPH OF THE PLACEHOLDER CONTENT; CLICK INSIDE THE TEXT, AND YOU GET THE COMPLETE SELECTION OF THAT STYLED TEXT. AND BECAUSE OF THE AMOUNT OF PLACEHOLDER TEXT, WE WILL GET OVERFLOW, WHICH MEANS AN EXTRA PAGE THAT WE DON'T NEED. AT THE END OF THIS EXERCISE, YOU'LL SEE.

Feel free to write your biography, the travails of your shipwreck, or just a shopping list of things you'd like your rescuer to bring you. Experiment; explore.

Done? Good. Now let's add a new text block. You'll notice the icons at the top of the Pages window. Choose Text from the Objects icon's pull-down menu. A new text block will appear.

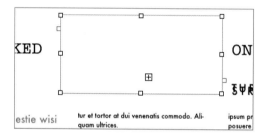

This is not just a plain old text block, however; if you look closely, it automatically moved any other text it may have overlapped. In other words, this text block appears to have a text wrap applied. To the right of the Objects icon is the Wrap icon. If that icon is grayed out, click any other object on the page and then click inside the new text block to select it. Its resize anchors will appear.

Notice that the Wrap icon becomes serviceable. Try each of the different choices, and watch the results on the surrounding text.

Enough of that. Inside the text block, type the subhead (SHIPWRECKED ON A DELIGHTFULLY DESERTED ISLAND). Here's where it gets good. Choose View > Show Styles Drawer. A drawer will open on one side or the other of your window, exhibiting a bevy of paragraph styles. We can also choose styles from the Style icon's pull-down menu at the top of the window.

Without even selecting individual lines of text, just click any of the styles shown. Choose one of the Mastheads, and the text will be too large; choose Body or Caption, and it's too small. Choose Heading. Sure, the text is still small, but we can remedy that.

This should be familiar to you now. Choose Format > Show Fonts. If you have room on your screen, watch your live text as you click different font selections. The text changes dynamically with each typeface you light upon.

Call me boring, but I'm pretty much sold on American Typewriter, 18 point. It gives us that utilitarian feel. Close the Fonts palette. Go back to the Styles Drawer, and click the arrow to the right of our Heading style. Now choose Create New Paragraph Style from Selection. Name the style something that helps you remember it—AmericanType18, for example. It's a good idea to name styles after one or two of their features. It makes it easier in the future to know what you're looking for at a glance.

Resize the text block by grabbing one of the anchor points and dragging it across the page.

Let's add our other Beach image now. Once again, there are two ways to achieve this: Choose Insert > Choose, or open a Finder window, locate the file, and simply drag it on your page.

Move the image around the page, and watch the text below. Yep—text wrap again. OK, enough fooling around. Resize the image to fit in the left column of the text block on the left. Put it snugly in the bottom-left corner.

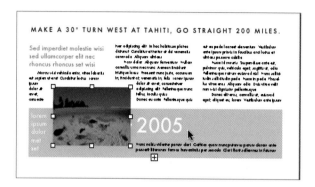

Notice the balance of the page now. In the top portion, we have an entry point of a solid-color field, with a banner message (HELP), and adjoining it, a beauty shot that defines the tone or voice of the piece. At the bottom, we reflect that relationship, but in reverse and in a less pronounced manner—a conversation, you see. We need not shout throughout the discourse. We state our argument at the top and explain ourselves in a calm, considered manner at the bottom.

Drag across the text in the mustard-color banner across the bottom to select it. Notice that there was an inline graphic next to *2005*. Food for thought. Replace the existing text with our own. In deference to the tone of our new piece, we'll combine the call to action with the tagline.

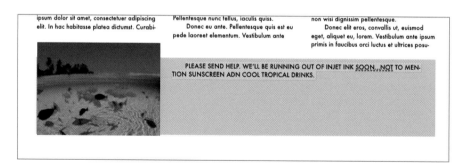

This time, apply the original Heading style from the Styles Drawer.

We have one thing left to do: directions. But let's mix up the layout this time. Choose Objects > Text to put a new text block on the page. Click outside the new block and then back in it. Nestle the new text block below the SHIPWRECKED line. Now type the directions (Make a 30° turn west at Tahiti…) and select Subheading from the Styles Drawer. The text is way too small.

Choose View > Show Inspector or just click the Inspector icon at the top of the window. On the Inspector palette, click the *T* (for Text). Now go to Spacing, and move the Character slider to the right until the line on the page fits snugly from left to right.

Stretch the line above to match it, using the same method. It should be no more than 2% character spacing.

Turn off Layout view, and assess your page. Make adjustments as you can to the central two lines to balance them between the graphics above and the three-column text below. Because we started with a newsletter template, there are some residual artifacts we should clean up now. We want only one page, so if any overflow text created a new second page, we'll have to delete it. Scroll down below your page. If there is a second page, select and erase any of the extra text, or just rewrite your content so that it fits. When there is no more content on that second page, the page disappears, and we are back to our intended one-page rescue note. Save the file.

Does the page get your message across? Is it inviting? Will someone come to the rescue? These are all questions we have to ask ourselves as part of the design process.

Sometimes, achieving good design is like making a good sauce. You add all the ingredients—a pinch of this and a pinch of that—and you simmer over a medium flame. If you're impatient, you'll taste it after only a few minutes. Sure, it will taste fine. But if you wait, let it go for a few hours, cover it, and forget it for half a day, it somehow gets better. (Or not.)

Design sometimes needs time to simmer. This is more important than ever if we consider the speed of the computer and the ease with which we can change things. Long before the digital revolution, inks had to dry, vellum had to be overlaid, and pencils still left telltale marks even after erasure. All these things let us slow the process enough for digestion and consideration.

So take a break from what you think you've finished; come back to it in an hour or a day. Come back to it with fresh eyes, as the saying goes. Then consider your page's merits.

Now ask these questions: Does the page get your message across? Is it inviting? Will someone come to the rescue? Would *you?* Does your eye flow naturally along the page, taking in each element in turn? Do you get stuck anywhere or tend to skip past any elements?

When you're new to the design game, it can be difficult to judge how well a particular design works. Let's try a different approach to give ourselves a basis for comparison.

We'll build another flier with Pages, but we'll give it a different feel and use some additional features of the program.

Rather than create a new file from scratch, let's build on this one instead. Choose File > Save (or press Command+ S) to save the changes in this version; then choose File > Save As and name the new copy we'll be adding to. (A name like pages_flier2 works well, but if you want to be creative, knock yourself out.)

Make sure you're still in Layout view. Let's start with the HELP text.

Maybe having the text aligned vertically isn't the most effective design approach, so let's rotate the text so it reads right.

Rotating objects in Pages is not the most intuitive of interface commands.

Select the text block, and open the Inspector. Click the small ruler icon (the sixth icon from the left). This is known as the Metrics Inspector. At the bottom of the palette, you'll see a rotation wheel. Grab hold of this wheel and turn it while watching the selected text. Voilà—she is right-reading. You could always just type 0° in the Angle window, but turning the wheel is so much more fun. Besides, you're on a desert island. What else have you got to do?

If some or all of your HELP headline disappears when you let go of it, don't panic; it's just *behind* the other text-wrap-enhanced objects on the page. Without clicking your mouse anywhere, choose Arrange > Bring to Front. If you clicked somewhere else already, just click the area where the HELP text was when you let go of it. You'll know you've got it when the rectangular border of its text box is highlighted in gray.

Now delete the green field to the left. Resize the Beach image to fill the page from left to right margin. Center the HELP text above the image. Pages helps you align images as you work with them. Notice the blue guide line as you drag the image over the center.

Drag the small text that says *STRANDED AND NEED TO BE RESCUED* just to the right of the *P* in *HELP*.

Now enlarge RESCUE ME to as close to 7˝ across as you can. You can gauge its length as you drag by reading the informational numbers that appear during the process. Center the RESCUE ME graphic below HELP, in front of but near the bottom of the Beach image.

Open the Inspector. We're about to see some of the more advanced graphic features of Pages. Click the Graphic icon in the Inspector (fifth from the left).

Select the Beach image. Now slide its Opacity slider to 60%.

Select the RESCUE ME graphic. Check the Shadow check box in the Graphic Inspector, and reduce its opacity to 60% as well.

Now for some fun. Select HELP. In the Graphic Inspector, there is a Fill pull-down menu. Choose Image Fill from the menu. Now choose the very same Beach grab you're using now. The text box should fill with a offset replica of the Beach image.

Notice in the Inspector the thumbnail version of the image and, next to it, another pull-down menu. Click that pull-down menu, and change it from whatever it may be now to Original Size.

In the Inspector, click Shadow. We're not finished. Now double-click the HELP text. With the text selected, choose Shadow again in the Inspector. We may have lost the STRANDED AND NEED TO BE RESCUED text behind the HELP graphic. Click the text, and choose Arrange > Bring to Front.

At the bottom of the page, drag the smaller Beach image over to the center column. Notice that the text abutting the image reconfigures to separate into two columns automatically. Click the mustard-color field. In the Graphic Inspector, change the color fill to crimson. Choose View > Hide Layout.

We can stop here and print our new and improved flier. But is it really new and improved? Have we made it more complex, but not better? These questions should always be on our mind.

This is part of the process: All too often in a tutorial or a seminar, you'll learn only the narrow path that leads to a specific end. If you tread just a hair to the right or left, you get lost, with few markers to get you back to a safe place. This is especially true in technology-based design.

So let's take a step back now and assess what we've done. Hmmm. Maybe in this case, we did go a little too far. Drop shadows, opacities, color fields—it's all too much. And too much can often ruin a good concept. In this case, I think we may have strayed from the path of good concept and good design, and wandered into the dark woods of "Look what I can do with this tool!"

Frankly, we can overdesign with almost any tool. The power of this tool, Pages, sometimes makes it that much simpler to go too far. If Apple-Works is the Little Engine That Mostly Can, maybe Pages is the Little Engine That Can Do Too Much.

Earlier in the book, we discussed how design is also process. Our Out-of-the-Box fliers made with TextEdit and AppleWorks showed very basic process-oriented design. When we employ the prepackaged design templates, the process is not as apparent, but it never loses its importance. So let's reverse-engineer this page and see if we can't strip it down to just *what works*. Simplify; take your time; consider your intentions.

Switch to Layout view. Select the background Beach image. Delete it. (Go ahead. It's all right.)

Now select the word HELP (double-click the text). Increase its size to 144 point (Format > Font > Show Fonts). Move the STRANDED text to the white space to the right, aligning it with the bottom of the embedded image in the HELP text block.

Select RESCUE ME, and increase its opacity to 100%.

Remove all the small content below the directions.

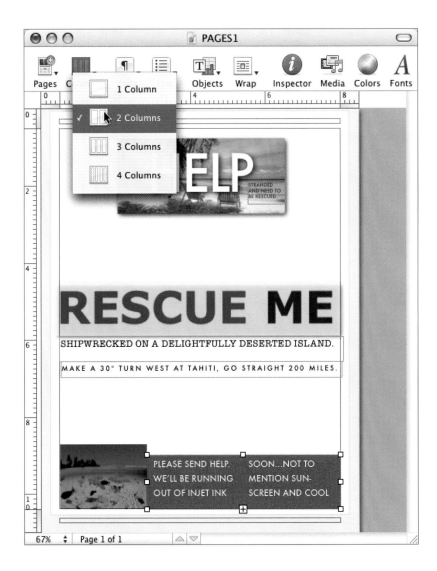

Slide the smaller, centered Beach graphic in the vacant space above. Now select the red text area containing the call to action. At the top of the window, click the Columns icon, and select 2 Columns. Now insert your cursor just after the ellipsis (…) in the text, and press Return. That should balance the text in the columns.

Save your file, and open your original Pages flier. Look at them side by side onscreen, or print them and place them next to each other.

With our second design, we applied—and then backed off from—some of the fancy design elements Pages makes possible. We also stripped away several elements in the template—elements that worked well in a newsletter design but weren't necessary for our flier. By choosing the elements that served our message and discarding those didn't, we ended up with a simple, direct expression of our message. It sort of reminds you of another flier we did, doesn't it? Yet with the addition of drop shadows, resized images, and a color field, it's anything *but* primitive.

By combining many of the same elements, we've produced a pair of distinctly different fliers, each well-balanced and effective but with its own flavor.

That means it's time, once again, to consider our target audience. Which do you think will be more appealing to our target audience? Back on the mainland, we might have the luxury of getting others' opinions and even floating the designs past potential rescuers. But ultimately, when survival is at stake, there are no hard rules to follow—just decisions to make.

Section 2: The Postcard

Postcards are a great, inexpensive medium for spreading a message. The postcard's role in our campaign will be to drive home the message we put forward in the flier. As a follow-up to our original message in a bottle, reaching out to our rescuer base, postcards will repeat and reinforce our message. They'll remind potential rescuers that we're still out here on our enticing tropical hideaway, ready for them to come rescue us. It will also let them know we're getting a little thirsty.

In terms of message, the postcard is a natural extension of the flier; you can even think of it as a mini-flier. From a design standpoint, the postcard differs from the flier in several ways. Some differences are obvious, but we're considering them now as designers, so let's consider them in turn.

First and foremost is size. The main design challenge with a postcard is conveying a message in a minimum of layout space. (It isn't a big concern here in castaway land, but we'll be optimistic and keep our postcard dimensions within U. S. Postal Service limits for postcard dimensions of 4.25″ x 6″.)

Another difference is the orientation of the layout. Our flier layout has what's commonly called *portrait* orientation—taller than it is wide. The postcard has *landscape* orientation—wider than it is tall.

The postcard has another attribute we didn't have to consider for our flier designs: It's interactive. The viewer can flip it over—and our design should try to make sure he does—to get the full benefit of our message. (OK, you *could* design one side of a postcard in reverse type so a viewer could hold it up to a mirror and read both sides at once, but that might not be the most effective strategy.)

Because you can't be sure which side of a postcard someone will see first, we must treat both sides as potential hooks for our audience. Each side should reflect and reinforce the other, ideally without being redundant. (It's hard to justify repeating ourselves when space is so tight.)

That's a lot to think about for such a small project, eh? Fortunately, the mechanics of creating a postcard on your Mac out-of-the-box won't tax your brainpower any further.

The quickest way is to use AppleWorks, which supplies a handy Postcard template. We should make our own original artwork for the template, but that won't be difficult.

Open AppleWorks. If Starting Points doesn't appear, press Command+ 1 or choose File > Show Starting Points.

Select Postcard. If no rulers are showing, choose Format > Rulers > Show Rulers.

A postcard is, of course, two-sided. AppleWorks' template conveniently aligns a two-up postcard, so that the front is on one page and the back is on the next. There is an inherent flaw in this two-page method of production, but we'll work with this method to completion. Then we'll make a slight variation in the mechanical setup for a second, more efficient go-round.

Before we start, let's put a new folder on the Desktop and call it Postcard. This way, we can keep things in order. You may want to take a moment to clean your Desktop before you begin, because the first thing you are going to do will require a clean open space on the Desktop (the one on the computer, not the one you're sitting at).

So let's get things started. We want to replace the rather pedestrian artwork of the template with something more modern. If we're continuing with our deserted-island premise, we might want something water-related. (You're probably getting a little tired of those Beach grabs by now.).

Open System Preferences. Select Desktop & Screen Saver.

In the left pane, choose Nature. Choose one of the water images. Notice that your Desktop background has changed to match it. Don't panic—you can always return to your original Desktop image later, if you need to.

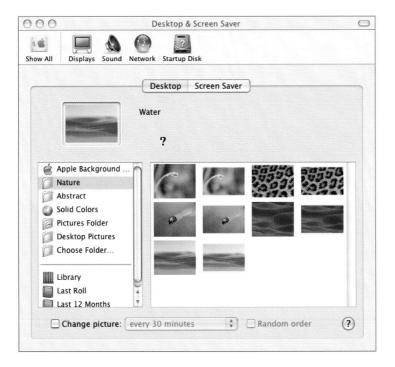

This little exercise assumes that you're using Mac OS 10.3 or later, because we're going to employ Exposé. If you're still running Mac OS X 10.2, don't fret. Just clear your Desktop of all windows and icons before you take your screen grab. Otherwise, while you're still in System Preferences, choose Show All, and select Exposé. With our next move, we will employ Exposé's Finder-clearing function. Check out the keyboard triggers in the bottom pane of the Exposé window. Quit System Preferences.

Now you're back in the Finder or AppleWorks; it makes no difference. Press F11 on your keyboard. If your Exposé settings haven't been changed, all open windows will slide off to the edge of the screen, leaving a nice open field showing your newly chosen water Desktop background.

Make a selective screen grab of the water background. Be careful to make it large enough and in the correct orientation for our postcard (*read*: landscape).

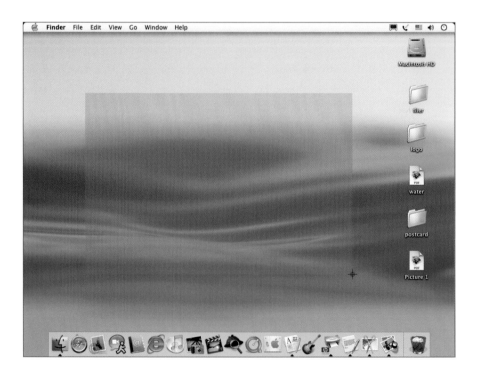

If you chose to use the basic selective grab (Command+Shift+4), you should see Picture 1 on your Desktop. Make sure it's the correct image by double-clicking it and previewing it in Preview. If it is as you hoped—that is, an image of water, with no icons or other distractions—save it and rename it Water. Now place the file in your Postcard folder.

Go back to AppleWorks. We are going to replace the simple existing image in the postcard with our new Water image. We can do this in either of two ways. First, we can go the traditional route, choosing File > Insert, locating our Postcard folder (Home > Desktop > Postcard), and selecting our image there. (Remember that in the Insert window, in the Format pull-down menu, you'll have to specify All Available.) The second method is perhaps a little simpler: Drag the image from the Finder directly into our AppleWorks Postcard window.

Depending on how large an area you've selected for your grab, the image will probably be larger than you need. Move the image so that you can locate one of the corner anchor points.

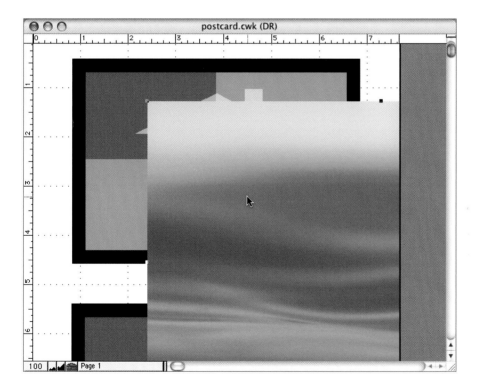

Resize the image so that it sits inside the black border on the existing top-most postcard art.

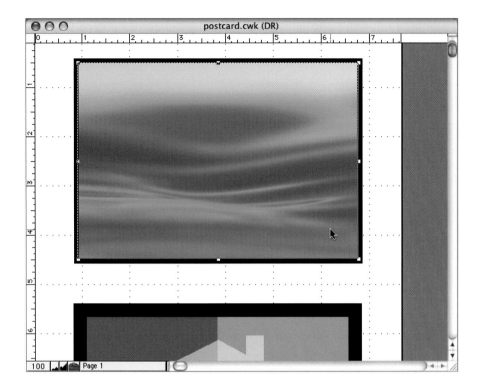

When the image is centered within the black border, choose Arrange > Move to Back. The image disappears. Now click the blue house graphic instead, and press Delete.

Oooh. Pretty postcard.

Select the text, and delete that. Select the Text tool from the toolbar on the left. Define a text area by click+dragging across the center of the postcard.

Type **Water, Water, Everywhere.** Select that text. Choose Text > Font, and choose an elegant but nonstandard font, such as Papyrus. Now make it 48 point (Text > Size > 48 point), and change the color to white (Text > Text Color).

There's a good reason for choosing a somewhat-exotic font. With a postcard, we must distill our message down to its essence. If you think of our flier design as a short essay on our predicament, the postcard is a declarative sentence. We don't have *time*, for lack of a better word, to be slow and subtle. Our message hasn't changed, but we have to condense and pressurize our layout to convey the message effectively in this new format.

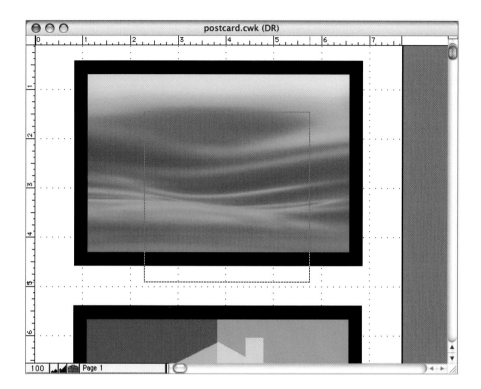

Using an exotic (but readable) font instead of a plainer typeface gives the postcard a point of view and sets a tone for the message. Most of this works in an unconscious way with the reader—and with you as well. Don't worry about explaining your font choice to anyone or finding the perfect font for any given message; that's not the point. If you experiment with the fonts on your Mac, keeping in mind the tone you want to strike and trusting your own unconscious reactions, you'll discover which fonts work with any particular projects.

NOTE: WHEN YOU'VE CHOSEN THE ARROW TOOL RATHER THAN THE TEXT TOOL, THE TEXT MENU DISAPPEARS. TO CHANGE THE TYPOGRAPHICAL PARAMETERS OF YOUR TEXT WITHOUT REVERTING TO THE TEXT TOOL, LOOK IN THE FORMAT MENU. YOU'LL FIND ALL YOUR FONT-SELECTION MENUS THERE INSTEAD.

The text will overflow slightly. Select it with the arrow tool, and reorient it so that it reads in two lines: *Water, Water,* and *Everywhere.*

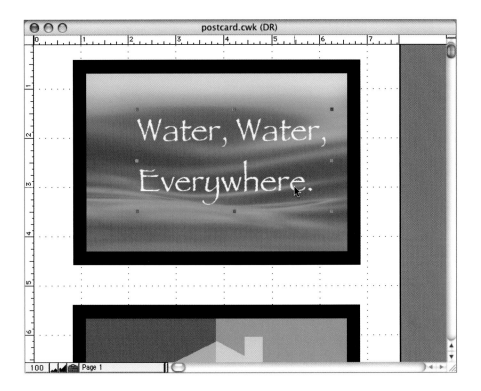

That takes care of one postcard front. Now we can copy just the new elements and paste them into the lower postcard front.

Shift+click the new text and the water background (without letting go of the Shift key, which lets you choose more than one item at a time). Choose Edit > Copy or press Command+ C.

Go to the lower postcard front, Shift+select its interior elements, and then delete them.

Paste (Edit > Paste or Command+ V). Drag the newer elements into position over the black border.

Choose Arrange > Move to Back.

We now have two postcard fronts.

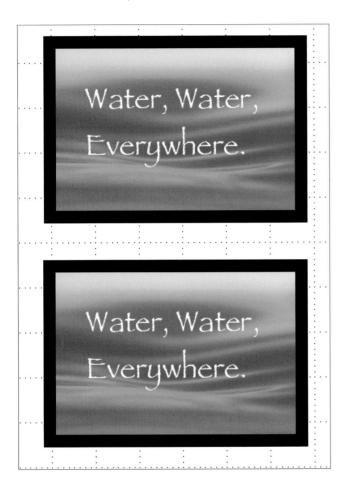

On to the postcard back. Scroll down to page 2. Just as we did earlier, we will work on the topmost postcard first.

Let's start by eliminating some of the elements that we won't be using. Select the text, the smaller house graphic, and the light blue field with the black border, and delete them.

You should have remaining only the blue-tone checkerboard border, an inner black border line, a yellowish stamp outline, and filler text for outgoing address information. Remove the address info.

Using the Text tool, define a text area that stretches just shy of halfway across.

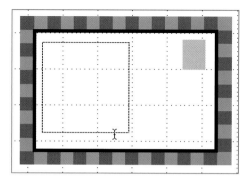

Type **Not A Drop To Drink**. Format the text as Papyrus, 24 point, black.

Now outline a second text area below that one, and type **Send Beverages Quick!** To save time in formatting the new text block, use the arrow tool, select the first text, and choose Edit > Duplicate (or press Command+ D). If you're in a hurry, there's an easier way to duplicate an object: Hold down the Option key while you drag the original. You'll notice that the original doesn't go anywhere, but a duplicate appears at the destination of your drag.

Either way, drag the duplicate below the original, switch to the Text tool, select the text, and replace it with the new content.

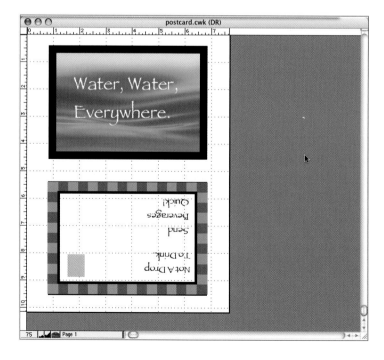

Now all we need to do is duplicate this artwork and place it on the other postcard back below. So repeat the process of elimination we used on the top postcard. Then Shift+Option+drag the two text blocks from above to the same relative position in the lower postcard.

Remember to be very careful not to move the borders at all; for printing, they must align with the front artwork. And therein lies the flaw in this sort of printing mechanical. To print two-sided, you have to print from page 1 to 1, take that page out, flip it over, reinsert it into your printer's tray, and print page 2 to 2.

Now let's remedy the two-page system.

Select all the elements of the top postcard back.

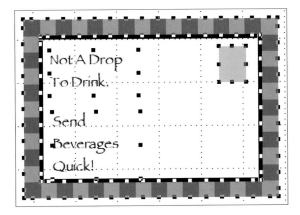

Choose Arrange > Group (or press Command+ G). Now drag the grouped elements straight up to the first page and lay them on top of the bottom postcard. Choose Arrange > Rotate, and in the subsequent window, choose 180°.

Now click *Water, Water, Everywhere,* and delete it. Next, click the Water graphic in the background, and delete it.

Choose Format > Document, and in the Size window, find Pages Down and replace 2 with 1.

Save your one-page postcard file, print it, flip the page over, and print again. It may take you a few tries to understand how your printer handles the orientation, but soon enough, you should have two two-sided postcards. Now find a sharp seashell and a straight branch, cut the postcards apart, and you're ready to mail them.

For a Few Bucks More

As you might expect, Pages affords more advanced methods than Apple-Works for making our postcards.

To get started, open Pages (Applications > iWork > Pages). From the templates, choose Moving Postcard.

NOTE: NOTICE THAT THE LAYOUT IS FOUR-UP AND USES THE TOTAL PAGE. THE POSTCARDS' MEASUREMENTS ARE NONSTANDARD, HOWEVER. WHAT THAT ESSENTIALLY MEANS IS THAT YOU CAN SEND THEM WITH REDUCED POSTAGE, BUT YOU WON'T BE ALLOWED TO SEND THEM WITH A BULK-MAIL PERMIT (MINIMUM SIZE FOR BULK MAIL IS 4.25″ X 6″).

Click the snapshot image in the top-left postcard. Choose Insert > Choose, and locate the Water grab we used in the preceding exercise. It replaces the generic house image but retains the outside snapshot border.

Now select the text *We Moved!* Replace it with *Water, Water, Everywhere.*

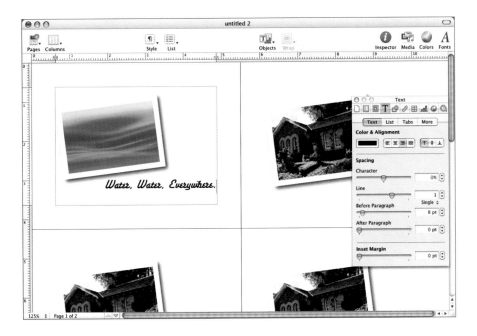

Carefully drag your cursor across the text. If you go too far, you'll notice that the image is also selected. Don't worry so much about that; it's an issue that refers directly to how the template was built.

Choose Format > Fonts > Show Fonts. Let's change the font from Santa Fe LET to another of the iWork-installed fonts. Try Bickley Script LET. Consider how different the postcard feels with that one font change.

Close the Fonts window. Rather than repeat the tedious process for each of the four postcards, place your mouse at the end of the Water, Water, Everywhere text. Click+drag all the way across (to the left) so that you have not only the text selected, but also the Water image. You'll know you have it selected because you'll see the anchor points around its perimeter. Now copy (Edit > Copy or Command+ C).

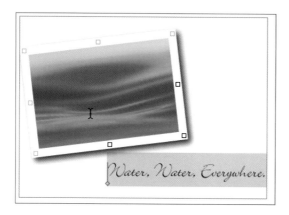

Now go to the postcard to the right. Select the text and image in precisely the same way. When those elements are selected, paste (Edit > Paste or Command+V). Your text and image, style, et al. should replace the placeholder items.

Repeat this process for the other two postcards. When all the postcards have new text and images, you might want to experiment with different typefaces in each of the four. See what different tones you produce just by replacing the font.

Enough of that. It's time to get back to work. Scroll down to the second page, where you find the faux-Latin placeholder text. Double-click the text in the left column, and type **And not a drop to drink. Send more beverages. QUICK!** You can replace the addressee information with a real name and address, if you like. Done.

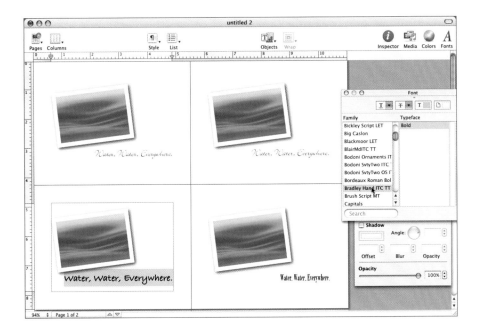

Once again, it's time to reflect on what we've created in terms of having satisfied our design intentions. Let's break it down according to our rules of thumb. First, our headline, as it were, is familiar to most English-speaking people. In its context on the front of a postcard, it shows a little humor and wit. It compels the viewer to want to know a little more (which means she should turn the card over and get the rest of the message). The use of a phrase from the world of poesy defines the target audience as an educated one. Further, it even implies that the rescuer should have a level of affluence (who else could rescue us and bring beverages?).

As for the relative functions of our layout elements, our layout and text clarify each other. Without the text, would you know right away that the image is one of water? Taking an image of water, without context, looking at it in a nontraditional way, gives it a level of abstraction—once again, intriguing for an educated audience. It works on the level of a puzzle. We all feel good when we solve a puzzle; we feel a small sense of satisfaction. If our layout works as a puzzle that the reader solves by simply reading the image and text in relation to each other, he feels intrinsically satisfied that he has solved the puzzle. He's on our side. In commercial design, if you can help the reader or viewer get on your side, you're halfway home.

Have we made our negatives into positives? Our repository of images is somewhat limited. But consider that with just one image and one line of text, you've intrigued your reader enough to turn the card over and read some more. Whether the reader is compelled to rescue us is the crap-shoot all designers take. But the odds are, at the very least, even.

If this last design worked, you should consider how you can change the various elements and see how changes in image, color, or text would affect the inner working and the outcome of your design. Try experimenting with another of the postcard templates. Open the Announcement Postcard, and after replacing the front image with your own, explore the Graphic Inspector's Shadow and Opacity options. Change the typeface, type size, and colors. Play. Then consider. But remember that a simple, direct approach is often more powerful than one that's too complex.

Now let's find some more bottles to send these off.

Section 3: The Logo

Flush with success after designing of our flier and postcard, we're confident that a rescue is imminent. So naturally, our thoughts turn to entrepreneurial opportunities on this barren spit of sand we now call home. Produce iPod cases from coconut husks? PowerBook sleeves from palm fronds? Phones with cheap built-in cameras that take and display blurry pictures on tiny screens? All ridiculous ideas that will never catch on.

Maybe we should concentrate on our design efforts. With our skills, we figure, why, we could almost make a living. But let's not get ahead of ourselves. If we're to take what we've learned on the island and make it useful when we're back in civilization, we'll need a way to identify ourselves in a professional manner.

We'll start by developing a logo and then work it into a business card design. We'll nail down a company identity so we can start doing business as soon as our rescuers arrive.

Logo development lives in a space somewhere between the practical and the preposterous. Some companies spend hundreds of thousands of dollars on a logo. Others ask their first vice president's 16-year-old nephew what he can come up with. Still others hire designers to help develop their commercial identity.

Logo design can be a profession in and of itself. But whether you're such a specialist or just trying to get a start in business, the process is pretty much the same.

A designer's customary first step in developing a logo is interviewing the managers responsible for the company (or product) the logo will represent. If the designer is lucky, the client already has a good idea of the characteristics the logo should embody. Frequently, however, the client needs help articulating what the logo should stand for. The goal of the interview is to help the client do so, and it should always begin with some fundamental questions: "Who is the target audience, or customer?" "What is the message (or impression) we want to convey to that audience?"

From there, consider how the company or product is to be viewed in comparison with industry peers and competitors: What are its unique advantages or benefits? What attributes set it apart? What kind of attitude should it project? By following these lines of inquiry, you can start to map out the fundamental characteristics the logo design should embody.

Do these questions sound familiar? They should.

Look back to our rules of thumb, and you will see that the interview goes through a process very much like the one we must go through when making any design decision.

The main challenge of logo design is also familiar, at least in concept: It's a highly intensified version of the task we faced when we stripped our flier message to its essentials for delivery on the postcard. With a logo, the distillation process is much more ambitious. Our goal is to concentrate the image of the company or product and the unique strengths it seeks to project and embed them all in a single representative symbol.

A logo is an identifier. It tells us something about whatever it is that sports that symbol. Sometimes, a logo is nothing more than a colored swash; often, it includes the name of a company or product. Many logos consist of nothing but type, stylized to convey the image of a company, brand, or even a person. (Recall a certain rock star with a passion for purple, formerly known by a funky symbol? How about an insurance company known by the signature of an early U.S. patriot?)

NOTE: THE TERM LOGO IS ACTUALLY SHORT FOR LOGOTYPE, AND IT IS RELATED TO THE GREEK WORD LOGOS, WHICH MEANS WORD. IN EFFECT, A LOGO IS A UNION OF TYPOGRAPHY AND FORM THAT SIGNIFIES A COMPANY OR BRAND. IT SHOWS US (MUCH MORE THAN IT TELLS US) WHAT THE BRAND REPRESENTS.

Type as Artwork, Words as Pictures

We can learn to see words as images. In fact, we must learn to see them so. Remember that exercise of unfocusing your eyes to see layout as forms? In the same way, we should practice separating type form from type meaning, if only for an instant. In a logo that contains lettering, type plays a dual role—as text and as graphic element. The letters serve their traditional role of representing words (or numbers, initials, or what have you), but they act at the same time as illustrations. When we look at a logo, the form, color, and proportions of the type are at least as important as the letters they signify. This allows a logo to *mean* much more than it *says*. If it didn't, it would just be a label.

The shape, color, and proportion of letters must carry as much of our message as the words, if not more.

For this exercise, our company will be called Crusoe. It says a lot about our situation and our outlook. We can be pretty sure we're not stepping on anyone's copyright; Daniel Defoe has been dead for a long time. And this is our island, anyway. Right? Here on our desert island, we're the designer, and we're the company leadership, so we have no choice: To begin developing the Crusoe logo, we must interview ourselves.

What is Crusoe? Crusoe is the culmination of our time spent stranded, foraging for food and eking out design skills, but also drawing inspiration from our lush surroundings. We're now *selling that experience* as a vacation. So we want the Crusoe logo to have a particular and definite personality. It should be simple and lean, like life on the island. It should have a classic nautical sensibility as well. Think of the America's Cup race. Most of all, our logo should exude confidence—confidence that our ordeal has made us stronger and that it has made us better equipped than anyone else to deliver desert-island adventures.

As we go through our design process, we'll keep these attributes in the back of our minds without taking them too literally. We'll try a few approaches to come up with something strong and modern, classic and inviting. Let's see whether we can do it.

Once again, before we begin, create a new folder on your Desktop, and this time name it Logo.

If you recall, early on I posited that typography and letter design should remain pristine—that we should rarely, if ever, distort fonts by squeezing or stretching them. The intention of the typeface gets lost that way.

But now we're talking about logotype, and that guideline no longer applies. In the case of logo development, we invert the original hierarchy of things. Earlier, the *readability* of the type and its *literal* meaning came first. With a logo, letter *shape* and its *graphical* meaning take priority.

We'll take three stabs at developing our logo.

First Stab: In the Beginning, Just the Word

A lot can be said for simplicity. Ironically, it seems, simplicity in design is often the hardest thing to achieve. Let's start with utterly simple text.

Open TextEdit. In the untitled document that opens, type the word **CRUSOE**, all caps. Select the text. Now choose Format > Font > Show Fonts. Choose Didot, 96 point.

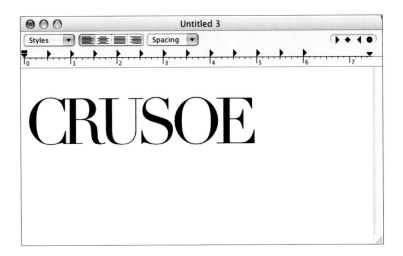

Select the text so that you see a blue field behind it.

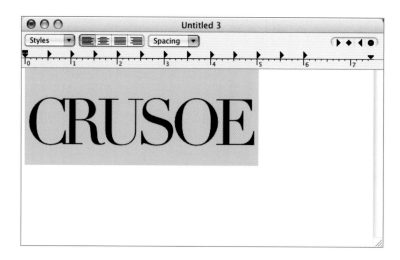

Back in the font palette, change the color of the selected text to white. Before you click the live TextEdit window, notice that the field is now gray. That's because it's not active. Make sure that there are no windows or palettes obscuring the text window. Now make a selective grab (Command+Shift+4) around the gray field. Try to keep your selection within the borders of the gray field.

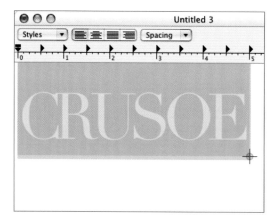

You have your first rendition of the logo. Now click the active TextEdit window. Make sure your text is still selected. The field should now be light blue. The text should be reversed out of the field in white.

Make a selection grab again, just as you did a moment ago. That will work as your second rendition of the logo. Save your file in the Logo folder on the Desktop.

If you would like to compare your logos, select both files and double-click. The Preview application will present itself with its drawer open, showing thumbnails of each image. You can toggle between the two images and get an idea of how they differ and which you may prefer.

In Preview, you can crop the image and export it as a different format. (Preview gives you an array of formats to export, from JPEG to PICT to Photoshop to QuickTime Image to TIFF, among others.)

Back in TextEdit, we can make some more changes. The obvious one would be the typeface.

Select your text, and change the font to Papyrus—a choice that should be familiar from our postcard design. In the logo, as in the postcard, the font's exotic nature and broken letterforms can reinforce the tone and meaning we're trying to convey.

If you like, you can also change the background color behind the text. Stick with the blue background that's already in place, or try clicking the color palette and applying the inactive gray field.

After you've decided, make a selection grab of the text.

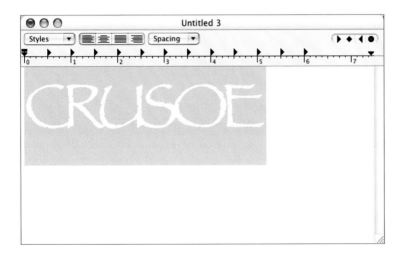

We'll use one more typeface and then we'll move on. Change the text from Papyrus to Herculanum. This font, like Papyrus, is what's known as a *display* font or typeface, intended for use in headlines, logos, and short lines of copy, in contrast with plainer *body* fonts or faces, designed for easy reading of long stretches of text.

Unlike Papyrus, however, Herculanum, is an *all-caps* display font. It contains no lowercase letter forms; instead, typing a given letter with and without the Shift key held down yields variant capital letters. Which brings us to the *U* in *CRUSOE.* This extra-wide variant is a bit extreme, so before you make any screen grabs , let's see how its lowercase counterpart looks.

If you prefer the narrower version, go ahead and make a selection grab of this logo. If you prefer the original uppercase version, return to it and make your grab.

Before we go further, you may want to explore color differences as well. Although the blue field from the active window limits what kind of contrasting colors you can feasibly use without distraction, the neutral gray that appears might open more possibilities. The most important thing to remember is that you should explore and experiment but always keep an eye toward simplicity.

We now have three logo candidates, all consisting purely of type against a colored background. Simple? Sure—but with the right design choices, that can be enough to establish a brand or identity. Just *try* to think of Kellogg's without envisioning its name as a red-script logo or of General Mills cereals without the "big G"—a logo consisting of one letter.

Second Stab: Shapes of Things to Come

Let's enhance our logos with simple shapes. Sometimes this method works; sometimes it becomes too much, and we find ourselves going back to our simple original ideas. It's a good idea to let things sit for at least a few hours, if not days, when developing a logo. Time has a way of clarifying our results. But who has that kind of time? Let's get moving.

Open the AppleWorks Drawing application. As always, show rulers (Format > Rulers > Show Rulers, or Command+Shift+U). We could duplicate our logotype-development process in pretty much any text-generating application, but in the interest of efficiency, we'll use the logotypes we made in the previous pages.

Insert one of your recent logotypes into the page (File > Insert) or just drag the file from the Finder to your open AppleWorks window.

Next, select the Rectangle tool in the toolbar. Align the crosshair cursor just above the top-left corner of the logotype. Now click+drag the rectangle across the length of your logotype, making sure that it doesn't go beyond that length.

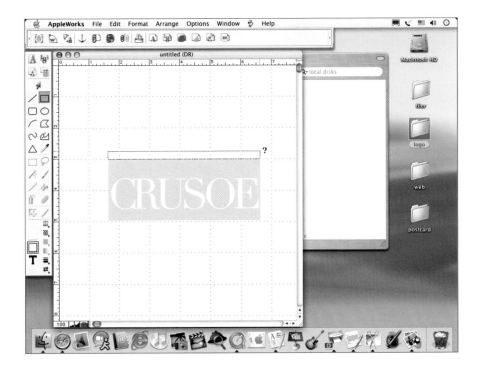

With the white rectangle still active, select the Fill tool from the toolbar and change the interior color of the rectangle to sea blue.

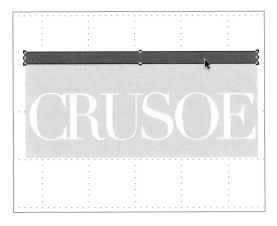

> TIP: **HERE'S A GOOD SHORTCUT FOR THOSE OF YOU WHO ARE SICK OF USING THE TOOLBAR. CHOOSE WINDOW > SHOW ACCENTS. A FLOATING PALETTE WINDOW APPEARS, DISPLAYING THE FILL, PEN, AND TEXT TOOLS ALONG WITH A FULL-COLOR PALETTE GRID BELOW THEM. USE THIS SHORTCUT WHEN YOU'RE CHANGING TEXT, LINE, OR FILL COLORS.**

The rectangle may have a black outline. Let's remove that line. Using the Pen tool, make the outline white.

The logo should have a blue cap now. The white line around the blue rectangle acts as a separator, clarifying the shape of our original gray field, balancing the top and bottom forms.

Next, select the Ellipse tool (that's the oval), and draw a 1″ circle.

> TIP: **IF YOU HOLD DOWN THE SHIFT KEY AS YOU DRAG WITH MOST APPLE-WORKS SHAPE TOOLS, YOU KEEP THE WIDTH AND HEIGHT OF YOUR OBJECT EQUAL; DOING SO HERE WILL KEEP YOUR "OVAL" PERFECTLY ROUND.**

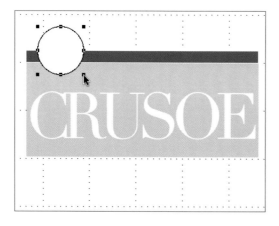

Using the same method you used to change the color and line of the rectangle, make the circle a setting sun, yellow with a white outline. Then choose Arrange > Move to Back.

Now use the Ellipse tool to draw a shallow oval to the right of the blue rectangle.

We can make this oval either grass green or dirt brown. That's up to you. After you've filled in the color and changed the line to white, deselect it.

Click your original logotype. Choose Arrange > Move to Front. Now move the oval so that only its top half appears and the rest is hidden behind the gray field. Make sure that the top of the oval just clears the height of the blue rectangle as well.

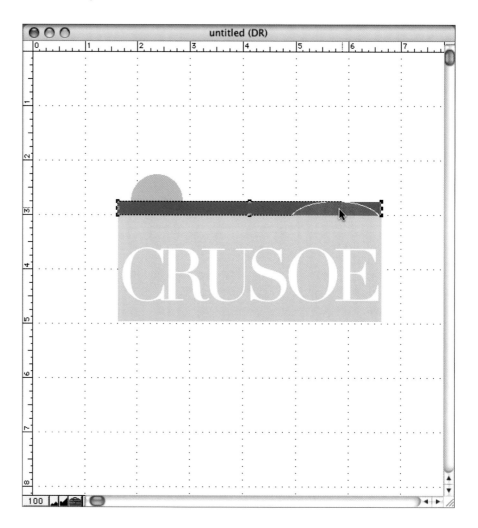

Now click inside the blue rectangle. On the right edge of the rectangle, click one of the anchor points and drag to the left until the edge is hidden behind the oval in front of it.

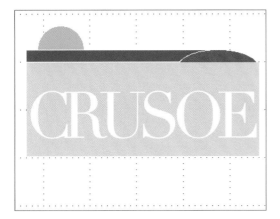

Now our logo is more than just type. It tells a story. But it's not finished yet. With the Text tool, just below the logo, define a text area the same length of the logotype. Type **DESERTED ISLAND TOURS**. Format the text to work with the original logotype. The example shown here uses Didot, but try Herculanum. Sizing the text may be a bit of an adventure.

By the way, if you are using a different typeface from Didot, don't panic. If you are using Papyrus or Herculanum, try Didot as the alternative type-face. Play with a few combinations, and trust your impressions of what works best.

But we still have to fit this text into our design.

You can increase the size without strictly designating a point size. Using the arrow tool, select the text. Choose Format > Size > Larger (or Smaller, depending on your need). The keyboard shortcut, which is the most effi-cient way of enlarging this text, is Command+Shift+. [period]. Replace the period with a comma to decrease. Try it first by pressing that keyboard combination one peck at a time. Now simply hold down those keys and watch as your text resizes dynamically.

Size the type to fit snugly and neatly below the logotype's gray field.

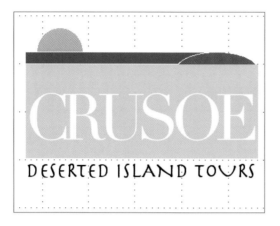

Save your file, but make sure to designate the file format. If you inspect the pull-down menu in the Save dialog box, you see many options. You can always save the first version in the native AppleWorks format, which will enable you to go back and edit it later. Then save in a different format, such as JPEG or TIFF.

We'll save both an AppleWorks and a JPEG (QT) version of the file. When you save your JPEG, keep the compression at Medium. Make sure to add the file extension .jpg, because AppleWorks won't do it for you.

NOTE: WHEN SAVING AS A JPEG, YOU'LL HAVE TO MAKE A DECISION ABOUT THE COMPRESSION OF THE FILE. JPEG (WHICH STANDS FOR JOINT PHOTOGRAPHIC EXPERTS GROUP, IF YOU MUST KNOW—NOTHING MORE INTRIGUING THAN THAT) IS WHAT'S KNOWN AS A LOSSY FORMAT. THAT MEANS THAT WHEN THIS FORMAT COMPRESSES A FILE, IT ALSO THROWS AWAY A BIT OF IMAGE INFORMATION. YOU'LL SOMETIMES NOTICE THIS IN FILES YOU SEE ON THE WEB; THEY SEEM TO HAVE HEAT WAVES OR BLOTCHES. THIS IS DUE TO THE AMOUNT OF COMPRESSION AND HOW MUCH IMAGE DATA HAS BEEN THROWN AWAY.

After you've saved your file, do one more kind of save, only this time, choose File > Print instead of File > Save. When the Print dialog box comes up, choose Save as PDF. Now rename the file with the .pdf extension. We'll do this for every version of the logo we want to save.

You should go back to the AppleWorks file and experiment by replacing the main part of the logo with other versions you made earlier in TextEdit. It's also very easy to go back to TextEdit and try out some new ideas.

Third Stab: Revert to Type

Here's another approach to the lettering. Again, this is a simple logo idea. But you've already seen that simple ideas can be enhanced (and, let's face it, sometimes ruined) with shapes and colors.

Open a new AppleWorks Drawing file. Using the Type tool, type **CRU**. I'm using Didot, black, 72 point.

Select CRU with the arrow tool, and Option+drag a duplicate to a clear space below the original. Double-click the duplicate, and replace the text with **SOE**. Now select it with the arrow tool again and move it so that it fits directly below CRU.

Again with the arrow tool, select the CRU element. The element is still type, so to change its colors, we'll need to use the Type tool. Change the black type to a cloud gray.

Select SOE, and change its color to sea blue.

Select the Rectangle tool, and draw a box over the two elements. With the rectangle selected, choose Arrange > Move to Back. Keep the black outline this time. Drag your cursor over all three elements to select them simultaneously.

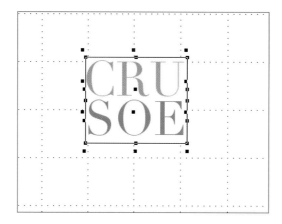

Choose Arrange > Align Objects. In the right column (Left to Right), select Align Centers.

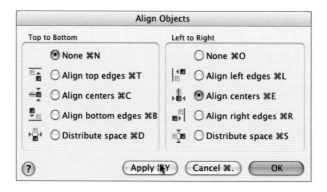

Click Apply. If the elements all look good and aligned, click OK.

Save the file. Be sure to give it a name that describes it. CrusoeStacked.cwk might do. After you've saved the AppleWorks source file, save it as a JPEG as well. And again, make sure to add the file extension .jpg , because AppleWorks won't do it for you. (Remember to choose Print > Save as PDF as well!).

Here's one last variation (we said this was a *process*, didn't we?). Go back to the AppleWorks file. Using the arrow tool, select SOE, and drag it over to the right and slightly up so that the *S* hooks around the lower part of the *U* in *CRU*.

Now resize the rectangle to encompass both elements.

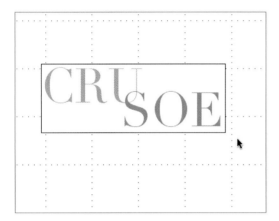

We can explore this shape further if we need to, putting a horizon line above part of the *S* and over the *OE*, and then putting a setting sun there again. Here's how. Draw a white rectangle over SOE, and make the line white.

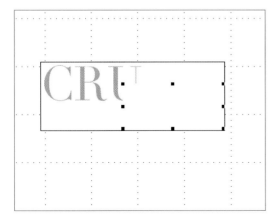

Now send that object to the back (Arrange > Move to Back). Next draw a yellowish circle (representing the setting sun) over the *O* and *E*.

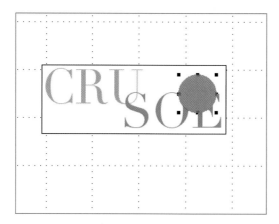

Send the orange circle to the back (Arrange > Move to Back). Now click the outer rectangle, and send that to the back.

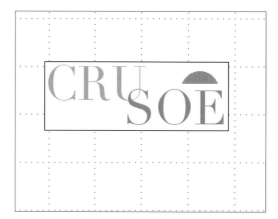

We can add the tagline text to clarify the logo, but for the most part, our design is done.

Annoying housecleaning step: Make sure that you've made a PDF version of each of your logos (Print > Save as PDF). As a matter of housecleaning, you may want to open the PDFs (you should have four, by my count) and make sure that they have no extraneous image info. They will, of course. But it won't become obvious to you until you insert them into another application. You will want to open Preview and crop the images to their essentials (see Part 1, "Read Me Next: A Basic Skill Set").

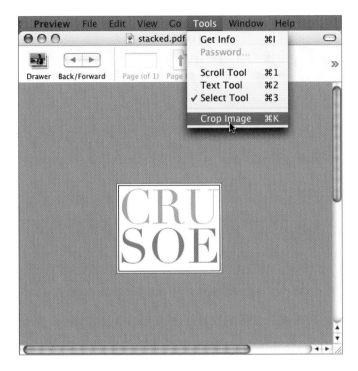

The fact is, these are just a few basic methods for developing simple logos. But by using the basic skills of screen grab in unexpected places—between gestures in the conversation, as it were—we can come up with some excellent results. Each skill can build on another, and elements can combine in surprising ways. The main thing is to be fearless about experimentation and exploration.

And of course, sometimes the best design decision is deciding when to stop.

We can stop here, look at our masterful work, and get ourselves prepared for implementing our fine design. Where is the best place to do so, you ask? Why, on a business card, of course!

Section 4: The Business Card

Our logo is done. We even have a few variations. Crusoe's company identity is crystallizing nicely. But a logo is no good unless it's widely visible. Someday, the Crusoe logo may adorn a fleet of corporate jets, but for now, we'll start spreading it around on our business cards.

As with our earlier projects, make a new folder on your Desktop, and title it BC (for *business cards*). We'll save our artwork in that folder.

The standard American business card measures 3.5˝ x 2˝. Of course, you've seen variations. There are trifold business cards that act as mini-brochures and oversize cards that double as bookmarks. But for the great majority of people carrying them, business cards of the 3.5˝ x 2˝ variety fit inside wallets and purses better than cards of other measurements.

The process of making a business card consists of two basic parts. The first is technical in nature, and the second is more subjective.

The first part is the setup. We'll make a template with a workable outline of the business card, along with crop marks. We'll set up our business card template with a four-up layout. That means we'll have four instances of our business card on one sheet. The main advantage of this approach is that instead of printing 500 sheets of paper to get 500 business cards, we'll have to feed the printer only 125 sheets. As you get more proficient at this, if you ever care to, you can fit an eight-up layout per sheet. But for now, we'll keep it simple.

A four-up layout is also advantageous to designers who can't make up their minds—or who want to experiment with options. There's no rule that says all four cards must be identical. You're free to put four different samples per page and, for that matter, free to use four different business cards. That way, you can choose the card that suits your mood, your sense of the person to whom you're handing the card, or what have you.

If you go that route, which is probably better suited to creative fields than to more staid professions such as finance or banking, you probably should limit the alternate designs to variations based on a single logo. A little variation in card design can convey a sense of flair, but deviate too much, and you're just being inconsistent—and undermining any distinctive identity.

When setup is complete, we turn to the actual laying-out of our card(s). This is really where the rubber meets the road, in terms of logo design. A logo that looks beautiful and powerful when you're drawing it in isolation doesn't always make sense when you implement it in the real world—sort of like the difference between conceptual art and paint on canvas. Ideas are easy. They're cheap. But you don't really know if you've got anything good until you put colors to the canvas. Context changes things. But don't worry—if a logo doesn't succeed in practice, you'll get a second chance to try adjusting it.

Using four variations of the logotype we designed in the preceding section, we will now design and implement four business cards.

Open your old friend, the AppleWorks Drawing module. Show rulers (Format > Rulers > Show Rulers or Command+Shift+U). With the Rectangle tool, draw a rectangle 3.5″ x 2″.

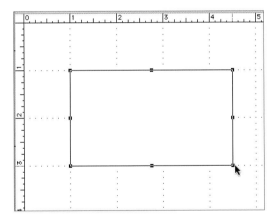

Using the rulers and the grid to guide you, move the rectangle to 0.5″ from the left margin and 1″ from the top. The right edge of the rectangle now sits at 4″ on your horizontal ruler.

Option+drag the rectangle to the right so that you've essentially mirrored it, the right edge of one to the left edge of the other.

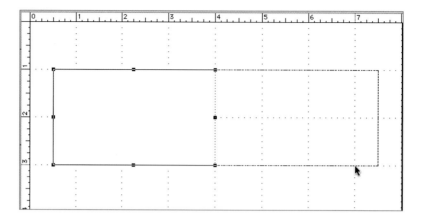

Now select both rectangles and Option-drag down, duplicating the pair so that the new pair starts at the 4″ point on the vertical ruler.

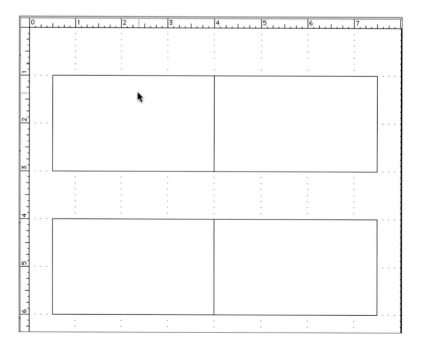

We won't always have these boxes on our artwork. These rectangles are guides for design. They won't be a final printed feature of the business cards. But we'll need crop marks to know where to cut our business cards after we've printed them.

Select the Line tool in the toolbar. Starting at around ⅜″ from the top, align your cursor (which should be a crosshair) with the left edge of the top-left rectangle. Drag straight down three ticks on the ruler (⅜″). You have just made the first crop mark. While the Line tool is still selected, Option+drag that crop mark directly to the right until you reach the 4″ mark on the horizontal ruler. If you have trouble keeping the line straight across, you can always *constrain* its movement by holding down the Shift key while you Option+drag. Now do it again with the crop mark you just duplicated, this time creating a duplicate at the 7.5″ mark on the horizontal ruler. It should look like this:

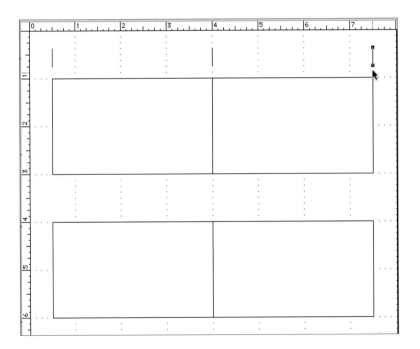

Now select all three of your crop marks, and Option (+Shift)+drag them directly down to the space between your two sets of rectangles. That accomplished, do it again, duplicating the crop marks so that they rest below the bottom pair of rectangles as well.

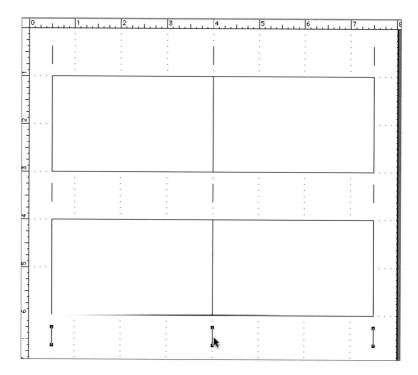

So much for the vertical crops. Now let's create our horizontal crop marks. As the song says, second verse, same as the first. Only this time, align your Line tool cursor on the 1˝ vertical ruler, and drag from the ⅜˝ tick to the left till you hit the zero point on the horizontal ruler. Now duplicate that crop mark down 2˝ to the 3˝ tick on the vertical ruler. Take both those crops now and duplicate them so they align with the top and bottom of the lower rectangles.

Next, select all four of the horizontal crop marks and duplicate them over to the right margin. Your page should look like this:

NOTE: THIS TEMPLATE PROVIDES US BUSINESS CARDS THAT ABUT RIGHT AND LEFT. THAT MEANS WE WON'T BE DESIGNING WHAT'S CALLED A BLEED. A BLEED IS USED WHEN WE WANT COLORS TO GO ALL THE WAY TO THE EDGE OF THE CARD. TO MAKE THAT HAPPEN, WE HAVE TO RUN THE COLORS BEYOND THE ACTUAL BORDER OR CUT MARK. THE COLORS BLEED OVER THE EDGE. IF WE WANT TO MAKE A BLEEDABLE TEMPLATE, WE'D HAVE TO SEPARATE THE EDGES OF THE CARDS SO THAT WE HAVE ENOUGH SPACE BETWEEN THEM TO RUN OVER OR BLEED OUR COLORS OR IMAGES BEYOND THE EDGES. IF WE WANT, THOUGH, WE CAN BLEED THE TOP AND BOTTOM OF THESE CARDS. FURTHER, WE CAN MAKE A BLEEDING FOUR-UP TEMPLATE BY UNLOCKING THESE ELEMENTS AND SHIFTING THE RIGHT AND LEFT RECTANGLES TO THE RIGHT AND LEFT ABOUT AN EIGHTH OF AN INCH, RESPECTIVELY.

Select all (Edit > Select All, or Command+ A), and lock everything down (Arrange > Lock). Now they won't move inadvertently if we somehow select them instead of our design.

You may want to save this file at this point as a template for future use. Choose File > Save As, and in the File Format section of the dialog box, you'll notice a choice of Document or Template. Choose Template. Your navigation window above will now automatically take your file directly to the Templates folder buried in the Starting Points folder inside the Apple-Works folder (which lives in the Applications folder in the house that Jack built). Name your file something like BC4up. Click Save.

The next time you open AppleWorks, this file will be among your prebuilt templates. Makes you feel powerful, doesn't it?

Here's another time-saving tip: In your original four-up file, choose File > Print. Instead of printing to your printer, choose Save as PDF. Now you'll also have a PDF version of the template that will come in handy in any number of applications. You can use this as a design sketchpad, if you like,

sketching out ideas in pencil before playing on the Mac. But more important, PDF is a standard image format that can be inserted into many high-
end graphics applications. Trust me, you'll get use out of it shortly.

OK, back to business.

The Design and Layout Stage

In the preceding section of this chapter, we created our logos. They
should be easy to find, because we were orderly and put them in their
own folder on the Desktop, called Logo. Right?

Now is the time to put them to use. We should have four different logos.
And because we saved them in JPEG format as well as PDF format, we
can easily drag them right into our template. So let's do that.

The logos may come in a bit too large, but we can resize the flat JPEG files
without too much trouble. The trouble with JPEG files, as we discussed earlier, is that they're lossy. So the images that we've so painstakingly worked
out will be fuzzy, and in many cases, they won't print as well as we'd like.

So let's try an experiment. Drag one of your JPEG logos into your template. Resize it to fit in the top-left rectangle. Now drag its twin logo in
PDF format into the rectangle on the top right.

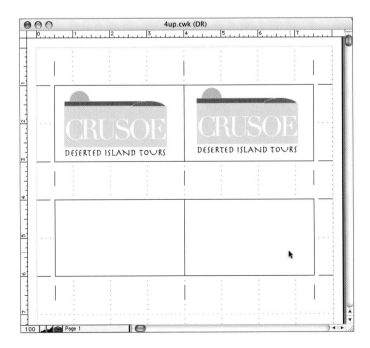

Now do a test print of the page. Take a close look at each image. The JPEG's edges—the curves especially—will show what we in the industry fondly call *jaggies.* The PDF, on the other hand, will have clean, smooth curves. This is specific to the differences in the formats themselves.

Which would you prefer to use for your business cards, then? You're almost certainly going to want the smoother, cleaner-looking image. So PDF wins. (In this case. When we get to designing for the Web, it's a different story.)

So let's delete the JPEG from our template and insert the other three logos we developed earlier in PDF format. (If you didn't remember to choose Print > Save as PDF for each of your earlier logo designs, you can go back right now, open the original AppleWorks, file and do so now. We'll wait.)

Resize each file you drop into your template. We want each to be no greater than half the size of each rectangle.

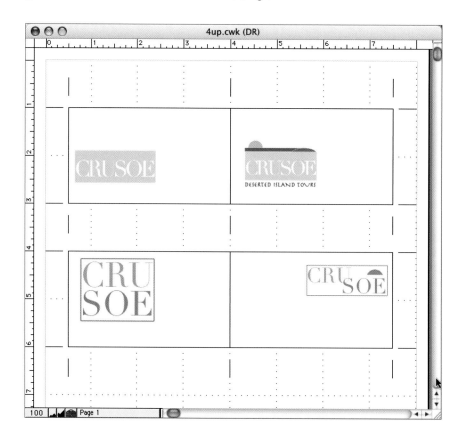

With our four logos in place, we can compare and contrast our designs as well. If you were to present a design to a client, this would be a simple way to do so.

Let's populate our business card with important information: name, title (if you have one), address, and contact info. It's a good idea to input each of these items separately. That allows you more design versatility.

We'll start in the top-left rectangle. Using the Text tool, position your cursor to the right of the logo (see the image above); then drag your cursor from left to right.

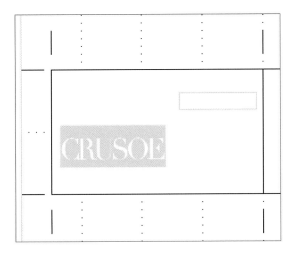

Type your name. Now select the text and format it. Experiment a bit; then try Futura 9 point. It works well, and here's why: Our logo uses the Didot font, a serif typeface, and Futura, a sans-serif font. We want to help the informational text stand apart. We never want other design elements to compete with our logo, so make sure the logo always stands slightly apart, as a separate entity. The logo is the *self* on the card. You and your personal information are just specific facets of the company's identity.

Using the arrow tool, duplicate the name text (Option+drag). In the duplicate, replace the name with your position or title. Repeat the process for the address line and contact info.

When you have all your information in place, you may want to shift the logo around to balance your design—maybe move the logo toward the top.

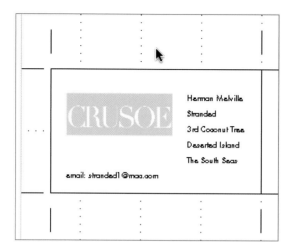

Now duplicate the information by Option+dragging to each of the other three business card rectangles. If you get tired of selecting each item, when you have all selected, choose Arrange > Group (Command+ G). It may be easier to duplicate the informational text as a unit. If you need to move an item in the group separately, ungroup the group (Command+Shift+G), and when you're happy with the placement, group the elements again.

Be sure to experiment with alignment as well as placement. Align the text to the right if it makes the card more balanced. Remember that you can always align the objects relative to their edges or centers. And although we haven't employed this technique, you can also ensure that items are equally distributed by using the Distribute Space option as well (Arrange > Align Objects or Command+Shift+K).

Before you print the page and glory in your genius, there's one final step. Select each of the rectangles, choose Arrange > Unlock, and delete the rectangles. Do not delete the crop marks; you'll want them as guides for cutting.

OK. Now you can revel in your genius.

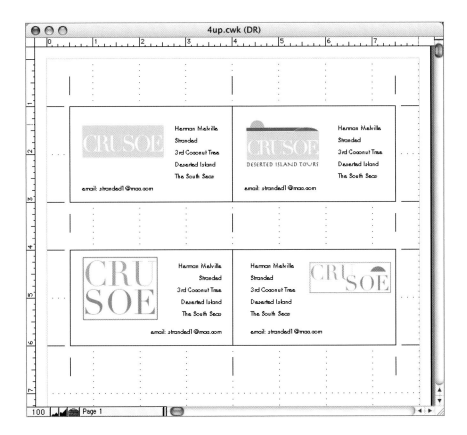

For a Few Bucks More

There's not much more you need to do to make your business cards than what you did in the preceding section. But the quality of the images, and enhancements like drop shadows and opacity changes, can make the difference between a good card and a great one.

We'll go right back to iWork for the next step. Open Pages. Surprisingly, among its myriad templates, Pages doesn't provide a business card. But that can't stop us. After all, we designed a logo with just a text editor, didn't we?

There's also little we need to do to improve our business card designs, so let's explore instead the ease of production we'll gain in Pages.

Choose the Blank page from the Pages templates.

Choose View > Show Layout. Now you will have the rulers, as well as the outline of the text blocks showing. But let's try something new. Put your cursor over the left ruler, and click+drag toward the center of the page. You should be dragging a blue guideline with your mouse. As you drag, a small yellow box denotes the guide's position in decimal inches.

Drag the guide to 4.25″, which is the center alignment of the page (a page being 8.5″ x 11″). Drag another guide, this time from the top ruler, and place it at the 1″ mark. Then drag one more guide 2″ lower, at 3″. Drag yet another guide 2″ lower, at 5″.

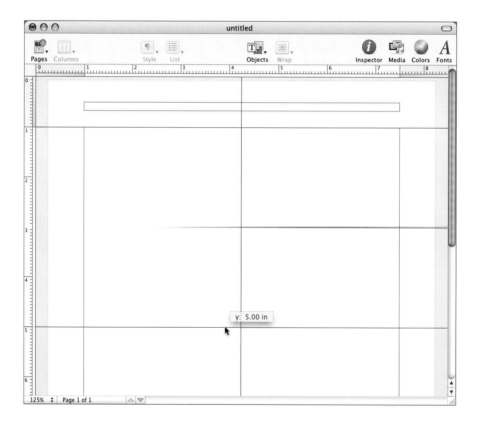

Now all we need are crop marks. Drawing crop marks in Pages is a slightly different process from the process in AppleWorks. First, make sure you have nothing selected—no objects, no text, nothing.

Choose Objects > Shapes > Line. A 2-point line at a 45° angle appears in the middle of your page. Drag the line to align with the left edge of your business cards. By dragging one of the endpoints on the line, you can change its angle and length.

If the Inspector isn't open, open it now (View > Show Inspector, or click the Inspector icon). In the Graphic Inspector, change the Stroke of the line from 2 pt to .5 pt. A 2-point line is much too thick to get an accurate cut (especially with the sharp edge of a shell).

Make sure that the line is now aligned with the 1″ mark on the top ruler but is not touching your guideline. When the line is in place, Option+drag to the center guide. Now repeat the procedure to the far-right margin.

Select all three crop marks, and Option+drag down below the 5″ vertical guideline. This all sounds familiar, doesn't it? You'll find that Option+drag is an almost-universal action in high-end graphics and illustration applications.

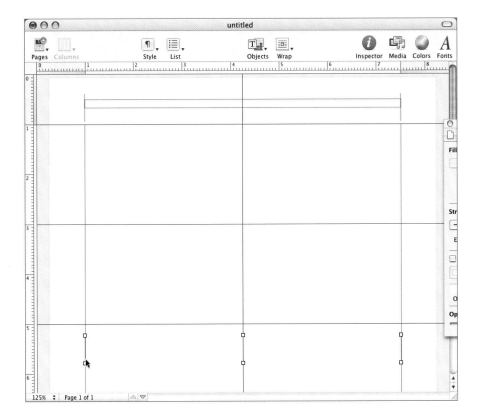

For the horizontal crop marks, you can select one of your recently con-jured crop marks. Copy and paste. Then align the new crop mark on the left side, along the horizontal guideline. It may be tricky to try to grab the crop mark while it sits on the guide line, so just select it, copy it, and paste again. Drag the newly pasted line to the middle horizontal guide. Repeat the procedure for the remaining crop mark.

When all three left-side crop marks are in place, select them, copy them, and paste them; then take the newly pasted three lines and align them on the right side.

It seems that the setup is always more intricate than the design itself. But why wait any longer? Let's get on with making the business cards.

The next few steps are the same ones we performed on our AppleWorks business cards. Go to your Logo folder, and drag the PDF files onto your page.

You can produce the same set of business cards that you did in the last exercise, or if you like, make a new set of layouts. Just be sure to keep the cards balanced, simple, and readable.

From Objects, choose a new Text area. Make sure that nothing is selected when you do this. If an area is selected, when you choose a Text object, Pages will automatically insert it wherever your cursor blinks.

Because you've installed Pages, you've gained some more fonts. You may want to explore some of them before settling on plain old Futura for your informational text.

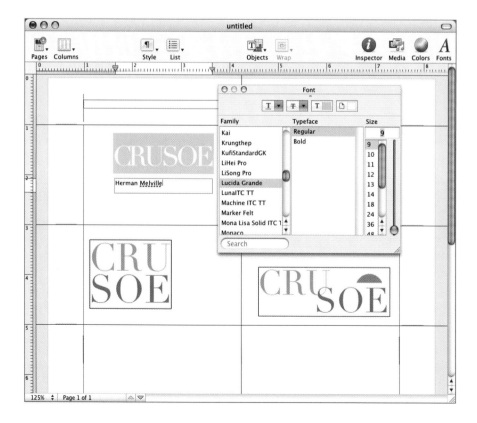

Remember to make each new line of text a separate object. Also keep in mind that objects in Pages wrap around each other by default. That means that if your lines of text get too close to each other, one or the other may seem to disappear. It's best to turn off text wrap (using the Wrap Inspector) before you go too far.

Duplicate the text items by Option+dragging and aligning them.

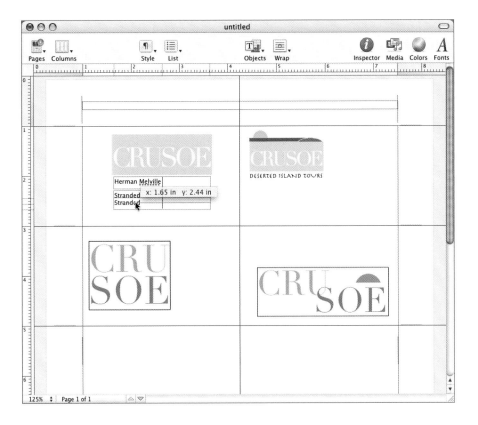

After you've populated each of your four business cards with text, play with the layout, make adjustments, and experiment with type and type sizes. You may want to have, for example, your name in 9-point Lucida Grande and the rest of the text in 8-point type. That way, the card has uniformity in style but emphasis on only certain items, such as the logo and your name.

At one point, you'll want to turn off Layout view (View > Hide Layout) and see what the cards look like without all the guides getting in the way. Because we didn't need the drawn rectangles that we needed in

AppleWorks (AppleWorks doesn't let you draw nonprinting guide lines), the cards may seem nude to you at first. But you can toggle in and out of Layout view to make sure of your design.

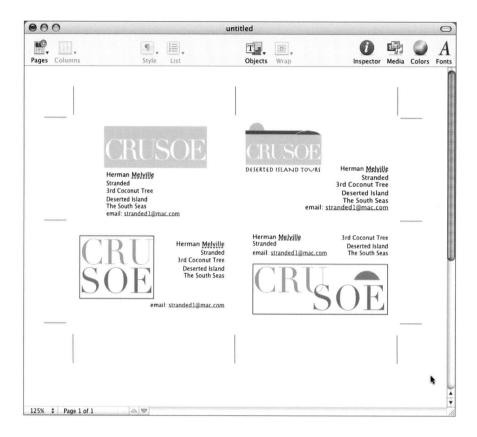

When you're satisfied with your work, print the cards. And do one other thing: Compare the clarity of your Pages business cards with that of your earlier AppleWorks business cards. Pages handles PDF artwork better than our more primitive applications. And it was a lot easier to make the cards, don't you think? So for a few bucks more, you're getting ease of use and lots of choices.

Pages folds many of the more mundane tasks into simple clicks. But more than that, the design examples we find in Pages are excellent starting points for inspiration and learning.

Feel free to steal design ideas from Pages templates; you paid for them, so it isn't theft anyway. Besides, that's what you're *supposed* to do with them. Emulate their designs and color schemes. Add to them. Throw things away. Be shameless. Be fearless. In the process, you'll reinterpret them and make them your own.

How Far Have We Come?

How far have we come? We've created fliers, postcards, business cards, and logos, using only what comes bundled with the Macintosh. Other than a few coconuts, we haven't spent an extra dollar on third-party software, Internet service providers, or output service bureaus.

The paradigm we've set up is a little extreme, of course. Odds are that you have a digital camera, an Internet service provider, and contact with the outside world. You probably even have a telephone. Yet you've created images using nothing more than the screen-grab function, the Save as PDF command, and a few relatively primitive computer applications.

Imagine what you could do with a digital camera, a scanner, or even a digitizing tablet. And let's not forget to mention a connection to the Internet. The images are out there. As long as we don't break any copyright laws, there's virtually no end to our creative process.

Wait—is that a sail on the horizon?

Chapter Two: Web Design

Famed graphic designer Milton Glaser once said that design could be described as moving things "from an existing condition to a preferred one." Let that sink in for a moment. Design is moving things from an existing condition to a preferred one. Nice stuff, huh? On a very basic level, of course, he's right. Think back on the work we did in the previous chapter. Aside from getting off the island, essentially moving from the existing condition (stranded) to a preferred one (back to civilization), we took the elements of our fliers and rearranged them from one condition that was satisfactory to another, more effective one. Then we sent the fliers off in bottles.

When Glaser made his observation, however, he obviously wasn't speaking to Web design. Most of his work precedes the advent of digital design anyway. And as such, he could not have been aware of the inherent bugaboos in Web design.

If there is one thing you must know about Web design (aside from the technical jargon and how to subsist on bad food and torturous hours), you must realize that this form of design is, above all else, a series of compromises. Finding that "preferred" condition is as illusory and ungraspable as getting a good deal on insurance.

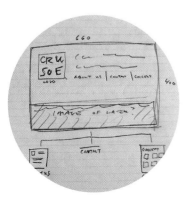

Compromises

In Web design, you compromise, compromise, and compromise. Pretty soon, you're either a good Web designer, or you're working for a global software giant we won't name here for legal reasons.

You must compromise your preferences for typography. Because your audience could be looking at your page on any type of computer monitor, or cell phone, or gaming console, you have no way of ensuring that your more exotic fonts will be present on any of those devices, let alone viewable as you intend them to be. You have to set your typographical aspirations low, using a system known as cascading style sheets, to get as close to your *preferred* intentions as possible. We'll give you an abbreviated explanation of cascading style sheets a little bit later on in this chapter.

You will have to compromise on color. In printing, your colors are limited by the inks you use and the ink color space you choose (TruMatch instead of Pantone, Process instead of Spot, and so on). On the Web, you have other limitations. Among them, you find that not every monitor is set to display as many colors as you, the Web designer, would like. One monitor could be set to display only 256 colors, while the next is set to display millions. Banding, hue variations, and downright different colors might appear. You said blue, and your viewers see purple. Beyond that, browser as they exist today have a limited color gamut. If you ever have the opportunity to work in high-end digital imaging applications, you will note that among the color space choices is a "Web-safe" palette. The Web-safe color palette consists of 216 colors. It's a variation on a familiar compromise we've all made at one point or another in our lives, only rather than *least*, it really is more aptly called the *most* common denominator. This set of colors will be consistently available in your basic, run-of-the-mill browsers, such as Internet Explorer, Safari, and Firefox. Colors outside that gamut will be *compromised* and adjusted.

Here's the reality of it: You will have to compromise your ideas about layout. The shape of a monitor, its orientation and proportions, and how much space your viewer's browser window takes up on that monitor all conspire to limit your grandiose ideas about how the pages should read.

Let's take a moment to invoke our Rules of Thumb. Consider our message. Consider our target audience. Organize and prioritize all design elements to express that message and reach that audience.

At this point, our message doesn't change, although it might as we get farther into the compromised nature of the medium. This harkens back to the idea of design as conversation. It's never fully realized but always moving, always shifting slightly. The much-quoted communication theorist Marshall McLuhan claimed that "the medium is the message." Well, that may or may not be true, but message and medium certainly do have an integral and intrinsic relationship. The characteristics of one bleed over into the other. We can't help that. It's just the nature of the environment we work in.

We always need to consider our intended audience. But now, with the Web, our potential audience size that has exploded. The Internet is the great democratizing agent of the age. Anyone with time on their hands can access the Web from virtually any country in the world for a fee that wouldn't buy you a cup of coffee nowadays, but it will buy you time on the Internet. So consider the audience and then be prepared to have that idea destroyed by the reality of the medium.

Still, we have to focus on our intentions, and the compromises and limitations we encounter in this medium force us to be more resourceful and creative. And this situation forces us to prioritize our design elements, to figure out what stays and what goes.

There are lots more compromises that we haven't mentioned that you will have to endure as you design your Web pages and your Web sites. But chief among the compromises right now is what tools you'll use to create your Web design and Web content.

The upside of this is that more applications than not contain some Web-centric features to help you get your stuff online. And believe it or not, some of the most sophisticated Web-design and -production applications are just text editors—big-city cousins of SimpleText—with specialized features that simplify production of HTML (Hypertext Markup Language), the code system that works as the skeleton on virtually every Web page.

That said, coding Web pages from scratch these days is an act of either technological nostalgia or stubborn geekiness. We don't all want to learn HTML, JavaScript, SQL database queries, and other nerdy protocols. Heck, even using the term *protocols* is tech-weenie.

Full-blown Web-design tools are beyond the scope of our out-of-the-box toolset, so we'll explore some *guerilla* methods of creating Web pages. And we'll try to keep the geek speak to a minimum.

In the arsenal of programs on our Macs, we have a few choices for Web design and production. In this chapter, we'll be using a combination of several. AppleWorks, iPhoto, Preview, Safari, and a digital camera will all have a hand in making our Web projects.

But first, let's go over some basics on the architecture of Web design and give you just enough information to make you dangerous to yourself and others.

The Russian Doll Architecture and Other Rules of Thumb

There is a difference between navigation and architecture. In many instances, designers and clients use these terms interchangeably, but this is a mistake. A Web site's *navigation* and a Web site's *architecture* are two distinct things. A Web site's navigation should be attuned to the way a visitor uses the site. The Web site's architecture doesn't have to adhere to the same structure. The architecture is a procedural stage in Web development. Like the architecture of a house, it's for building. It's structural. But walking through a house is not called architecture; it's called living. In a similar fashion, we develop a Web site with an architecture in mind, but we live in the site in a completely different way.

Let's consider the humble Web page. Although a Web site can consist of just one page, most sites consist of more than one page, and often hundreds of pages, all interconnected by one of the Web's signature attributes: the hyperlink. Links—in the form of buttons, pull-down menus, and hypertext—separate the Web from every other publishing medium. In a well-designed site, they allow visitors to hopscotch through hundreds or even thousands of pages to find relevant information within a few mouse clicks. Links help visitors find their way back home after exploring a site and enable them to connect from your site to useful information stored a continent away. Links make the Web a *web*.

Unlike a book or a movie (or a flier or even a postcard), a Web site has no clearly defined beginning, middle, and end. You can (and usually should) try to tell stories with a site—weaving message(s) into one or more "plots" that branch from the home page. But no matter what you do, some visitors are bound to link in to inside pages without coming in through the front door. You can tell a great story, but users—and the Web itself, via search engines and the like—tend to treat sites like reference volumes, to be dipped into where needed.

Our challenge as Web designers, then, is an amped-up version of the eavesdropper problem we discussed in connection with our flier in Chapter 1. We want every page of our site to be capable of grabbing a member of our target audience and drawing her in to hear our message. If a new Google link starts pulling traffic to a piña colada recipe page deep inside the Crusoe site, we can't expect every new visitor to become a potential customer, but that page's design should be compelling enough to make the rest of the site a worthwhile visit. Every page in a site is a potential entry point to a story that's already in progress. Site design should strive to make it easy for newcomers to get caught up and follow along.

That brings us back to that important element of Web design, the notion of navigation: how you'll present your site's contents to visitors in a way that communicates your message effectively and gives visitors (or at least the ones you really care about—your target audience) a good experience. Again, there's a parallel here to our discussion of the flier design. Site-navigation tools should guide a visitor through a Web site the way a layout guides a viewer's eye along a page.

As with all design considerations, our approach to site-navigation design begins with Andrew's Rules of Thumb (everybody, all together now):

1. Consider our message.

2. Consider our target audience.

3. Organize and prioritize all design elements to express that message and reach that audience.

By now, we've got our message down: Crusoe provides exciting, exotic, carefree desert-island excursions.

We're still waiting on the formal market research, but we've also got a pretty good idea about our target audience: folks with a yen for adventure, a notch or two more intense and driven than most. They work hard and have incomes to prove it, and they can't understand why anyone would want to *waste* a precious vacation by *relaxing* the whole time.

Which brings us to Rule 3, the one that really counts when we're planning site navigation. We'll think about design specifics in a while, but first, let's consider what content needs to be on the site and how we should organize it.

What do we want our site visitors to know (what's our message)? There are no rules for this stuff, and the answers for every site will be different, but here are a few logical answers for our hypothetical Crusoe site:

- What Crusoe does

- What to expect on a Crusoe Deserted Island Tour

- Who's behind it all (and why our castaway experience makes us the best choice for delivering a true-to-life island escape)

- How to book an adventure of your own *right now*

Now let's consider our target customer and the information he's going to *want* from the site. Again, there are no rules, but here's a stab:

- How much will this cost?

- Gee, that's a lot of cash. Can I get more information before I make up my mind?

- Do these guys have a track record?

- Is this going to be safe?

- Where and when do the trips depart?

Based on these answers, here's a stab at how to organize the site navigation in a logical way that conveys our message and addresses the visitor's concerns. The three main headings would be linked from the home page where they'd provide links to the appropriate subpages.

Home page

The Crusoe Experience (photo spread, links)

What to expect

Customer endorsements

Schedules and accommodations

Health and safety

Recommended packing list

About Crusoe (the tale of the castaway)

Corporate partners

Company history

Investment info

Book Me, Dano! (online booking info)

How to book a trip

Costs

More info

This is just one possible organization. Remember that there'll be cross-linking between sections and pages (the Book Me, Dano! page should be accessible everywhere). Also keep in mind that this navigation scheme may need to grow someday. Perhaps we'll add a line of Crusoe sports-wear or a line of travel books. Be ready to roll with the changes.

Now that we've got our site navigation figured out, it's time for a dose of reality: A site like this is a little too elaborate for us to build here step by step. And frankly, our out-of-the box Mac tool set isn't especially well suited to building one.

So we'll build a couple of sites that are a little less ambitious, to give you a sense of how pages link up and how text and images are arranged on a Web page. As we go through these simpler examples, remember that the same principles apply when you're building a bigger site.

Before we start our small site, let's take one final turn back to the consideration of site architecture. Think of the site as a building, with rooms and entryways. If it's a storefront, think of it in those terms. GIF animations, Flash video, and QuickTime movies are all art on the walls. But the architecture is the underlying thought that keeps the building consistent.

When designing a site, therefore, consider how you would like the site to be built (architecture), and as with navigation, plan it beforehand. Let's take a look at how this might work, bearing in mind that this is just one system (but one proved to work) and that different sites may require different approaches to site architecture. (You should also be aware that many professional site-design programs, such as Adobe/Macromedia Dreamweaver, take care of a lot of the site-architectural duties for you as you build and link your pages.)

A site architecture often begins with a scavenging run. Name a folder for the site (we picked crusoe_web),and fill it with all the raw material you have on hand for use with the Web site: your *source files.* In our case, these could include our AppleWorks project files, screen grabs, finished images, and so on. The folder probably won't contain everything you'll eventually use to build the site, and it'll almost certainly include some stuff you won't use. That's OK.

When you're done hunting and gathering, open the folder, and create a new folder called sourcedocs inside the crusoe_web folder. Place all the stuff you've collected inside sourcedocs. Create another new folder, inside crusoe_web and next to sourcedocs, and name it crusoe_site. This folder will hold our *processed* files, derived from the source files but sized and formatted for use on the Web page. We haven't processed any files yet, but we know we will, so we'll create some folders to hold them when we do: Inside crusoe_web, create two new folders, image_assets and sub-pages. The first will hold (you guessed it) processed image files; the second will hold the (HTML files) for our "inside" Web pages. The architecture develops like a collection of Russian dolls, one nested in another inside another.

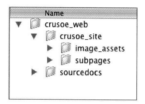

Naming files is crucial in Web production. The rule of thumb in this case is no uppercase and no spaces. A common mistake many Web creators fall victim to, however, while using this naming system is making image names incomprehensible. Too many numbers and nonmeaningful letters only make for confusion. A sample of most Web sites will give you names of image assets like header1_r2_c6_f2.gif. Even this is easy to decode, of course (a header image, located in row 1, column 6, frame 2, which means it's a rollover state). But who would want to? Try to keep names clear and understandable. Name things for what they are.

Naming things in this manner not only makes it easier for your Web projects, but also makes it habit forming. Soon enough, you'll find yourself naming anything you can with underscores, or ramming words together and ending them with three-letter extensions. (My wife had to stop me from naming our younger son erik_shalat.son.)

There are no exact rules to apply to file naming and folder nesting. These guidelines aren't set in stone; they are merely guidelines. The main thing is to stay organized and consistent in your folder-inside-folder-inside-folder system.

OK, now that we've got an architecture in place and some naming conventions worked out, let's start filling those site folders. We'll start by processing some image files.

There are a couple of reasons why this is necessary. For starters, Web browsers universally recognize just two image-file formats: JPEG, commonly used for photographic images (which we've already discussed in the context of our print projects); and GIFs (graphics interchange format), typically used for simple line art, solid-color graphics, and images that contain transparency. Some browsers also support the file formats used for Mac screen grabs (PDF in Mac OS X 10.3 [Panther] and PNG in Mac OS X 10.4 [Tiger]), but in general, we'll want to convert screen grabs (and all other images) to JPEGs or GIFs.

In addition, source files, especially high-resolution images, are often far too large for use on a Web page. The bigger an image, the longer it takes to appear onscreen in a Web browser. Big files also consume more server bandwidth—an important consideration if your hosting service meters your use. Converting images to JPEG or GIF format typically reduces their file size significantly, often with little or no noticeable difference in image quality.

Even source files in the desired formats often need to be processed. A common example are JPEG images from digital cameras, which commonly weigh in at well over 1 MB and, if displayed full-size onscreen (they seldom are), exceed the size of most desktop monitors. Saving such a file at the actual size in which it will be used on the Web page can reduce its file size to a few dozen kilobytes. That makes for much snappier performance when viewing a page in a browser.

One more thing about using images in Web pages: Unlike in page layout, where we can resize our images on the fly, in Web pages, it's best to have the images the correct size before you place them on the page. If an image on the Web page is 250 pixels by 250 pixels, you'd better make your processed image that exact size. Otherwise, you'll get the one thing a Web design can't afford: unexpected results. (Unexpected results are to Web design what discomfort is to a doctor: pain.)

Also, as we'll soon see, exporting a Web page from iPhoto can take care of a lot of this drudgery for you.

OK, end of primer. Let's get down to making some Web pages.

Make a Page from Scratch

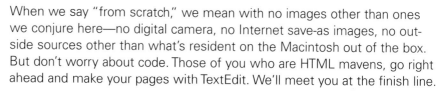

When we say "from scratch," we mean with no images other than ones we conjure here—no digital camera, no Internet save-as images, no outside sources other than what's resident on the Macintosh out of the box. But don't worry about code. Those of you who are HTML mavens, go right ahead and make your pages with TextEdit. We'll meet you at the finish line.

More than any other form of digital design, Web design requires you to do your prep—to collect as many of your images and as much of your content as you can before you begin the actual Web-page production. It's always a good idea to sketch your design on a piece of paper before doing anything else. Many designers also sketch a sort of flow chart that describes the architecture of the page-to-page relationships. But we'll keep this simple.

We'll design a home page first. Then we'll add an About Us page and a link to a photo gallery. It will be pretty primitive, so let's not get our hopes up. For some reason, Web design out of the box is the most difficult aspect of the whole bundle.

If you understand the fundamentals, you can use them as building blocks to create more complex projects later. Too many design novices jump into the fray, damn the torpedoes. And though they may get something on the Web, it's rarely reusable, scalable, or (dare we say it?) good.

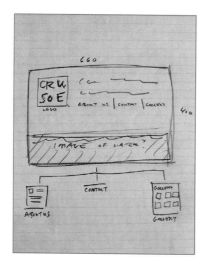

So create a very basic outline of how many pages we're going to have, the tiered system or hierarchy of the subpages, and the contact and navigation links on each page.

When you're proposing a site to a client, it can only help to create elaborate and specific site-plan sketches with the client, in pencil, before you put mouse to HTML editor.

There are other considerations beyond the site sketch that you'll want to think about, of course. Let's keep this as simple as we can and move forward to discuss those compromises…uh, I mean considerations.

Because the majority of browser windows open with 800- x 600-pixel windows, we'll use those dimensions as a starting point. We can't fill that whole area up with content, however, because we need to compensate for all the other stuff you find on a browser window—toolbars, menu bars, and so on. We want our home page to be completely readable at a glance. Subsequent pages can scroll down *below the fold,* but your home page should be complete within the browser window. So to be safe, we'll give our home page a 660- x 400-pixel setup.

The notion of content appearing *below the fold* on a Web page comes from another, older publishing field: the world of newspapers. In newspaper layout, you have a subtle hierarchy of importance on a front page. The most important articles are *above the fold*—that is, on the upper half of the page. When you buy a newspaper, it doesn't come in a large flat sheet; it's folded, at the very least, in half. There's an upper half, and there's a lower half. When the paper is lying in a pile or on a rack, you see the upper half. That's the above-the-fold half. That's the selling half. That's the home page.

When we design a home page, we don't have to put everything in the site on it—just the most important stuff. We can just think of it as our *above-the-fold* content—and to extend the newspaper analogy, think of it as home for our top headlines and one or two compelling images. In "analog" newspapers, part of the space above the fold is dedicated to subheads and the lede paragraphs of the top stories, but clickable hypertext headlines are often all that's needed on a Web page.

In fact, when you have a chance, go to the home page of your favorite newspaper. You won't get the whole article right there on the front page. At the very most, you'll get a headline and an abstract, or *lede* [sic] *graf.* (That's journalism talk for the first lead paragraph of the article.) It's meant to tease you into reading further by explicitly stating the subject matter, point of view, and position of the article.

OK, where were we? Right. Our home page's core content—text, head-lines, and images—must fit in a usable area 660 x 400 pixels.

We'll take that into account when we size our images. We'll get to some of our famous screen grabs soon, but first, let's take a different tack. Here's a neat way to access all the Desktop-background images that come with your Macintosh without making any screen grabs.:

1. Open iPhoto.

   The default library will be empty unless you've already added images of your own. Let's pretend you haven't yet.

2. Choose File > Add to Library (Command+O).

3. Navigate to Macintosh HD/Library/Desktop Pictures.

4. Click OK.

The iPhoto library will now populate with every Desktop image that comes with your Macintosh. If you don't want one or any of the images you've just imported, you can delete them from the library by selecting the image(s) and pressing Delete on your keyboard. Don't worry—the images won't be missing from the original Desktop Pictures folder. iPhoto copies the images into its own folder. So you're getting rid of only the copies in the iPhoto folder, not the originals.

Referring to the sketch, we will need at least two images to start. The first is our logo, and the second is a look-and-feel image. If we go back to our previous lesson, we can retrieve one of the logos we created.

This is a quick way to get access to a lot of abstract images fast.

While we're in the mood to gather images, let's locate the JPEG version of the logo we created in Chapter 1. For this exercise, we'll use the stacked logo. Choose File > Add to Library (Command+O) to add the logo to your iPhoto library.

To make things easier in the future, make a new album in iPhoto. Click the plus sign (+) in the bottom-left corner of the iPhoto window. Name the album Crusoe. Now let's drag a few of the images we might want to use for our Web pages into the newly created iPhoto album. Select the images you like by Shift-clicking or Command-clicking, and drag them over the small book icon on the left to populate the album.

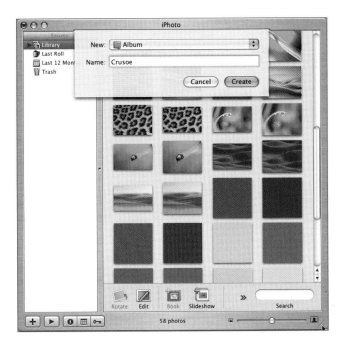

Now click the album name, and only those images you've chosen will show in the main window. Choose one of the images. We'll use this image as the bottom image in the Web page (refer to your sketch). Double-click the thumbnail of the image. It opens the image in a new edit view.

iPhoto gives us several useful editing tools. We can change the color of an image or remove the color altogether. We can do basic image cleanup or enhance the contrast, saturation, and exposure. We can straighten images that are askew and rotate images. And, of course, we can crop images.

If we weren't sure of our final sizes, we could just crop our source images for content now and resize them when we export them from iPhoto. We have a pretty good idea of what we need now, so we'll go ahead and crop them to size.

Unfortunately, there is no ruler in the iPhoto window, so we'll be able to change only the proportions, or *aspect ratios,* of our images, not their specific pixel dimensions. But don't worry—when we export our images for our Web page, we can scale them to the sizes we need.

First, select an image, and use the Get Info function to determine its original dimensions. Choose Photos > Get Info; press Command+I ;or, if the Sources drawer that lists your photo albums is open, click the circular *i* button in the bottom-left corner of the iPhoto window. You'll generally want to be sure that the source photo is larger than the final image you're creating. If it isn't, iPhoto will have to stretch it to enlarge it—and the results probably won't be very attractive. (An exception might be an enlargement intended for use as a background image, where image detail isn't so critical.)

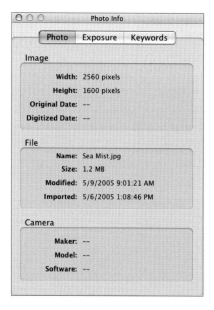

Double-click the image. When the Edit window opens, your cursor becomes a set of crosshairs. Click-drag the cursor across the image. What we're looking for is a strip of the image. This is difficult to do with any precision because we don't have a ruler, so take your time. If you've seen what they call letterboxing in Cinemascope widescreen movies, you will understand that this is what we're looking for. We're going to make the aspect ratio of our image a superelongated Cinemascope image.

When you're satisfied with the image, click the Crop tool; then click Done. Now select the image, and in iPhoto's bottom-left pane, click the Info icon. You'll see that the size information reflects the new aspect ratio.

For our purposes here, we want the image outside iPhoto. (Right after this, we'll make a Web page directly from iPhoto.) So with your cropped image selected, choose Share > Export (Command+Shift+E).

The ensuing dialog box give you three main choices: File Export, Web Page, and QuickTime. Select File Export.

Now choose JPG from the Format drop-down menu. In the Size section, select Scale Images No Larger Than, and in the text box for width, type **660**. The height will automatically adjust itself accordingly. Click Export.

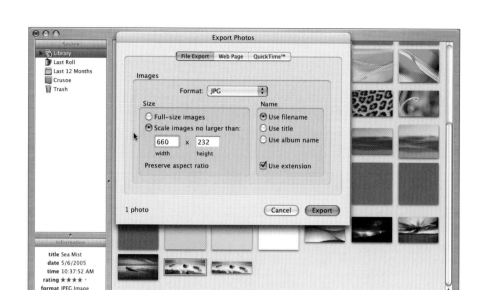

Let's rename the file according to the naming conventions discussed earlier. We'll be using this image as the bottom of the home page, so we'll name it appropriately. Navigate to the crusoe_web/crusoe_site/image_assets folder. After you click Export, in the Save As text box, name the file homebottom-landscape.jpg. If that's not clear enough, what is?

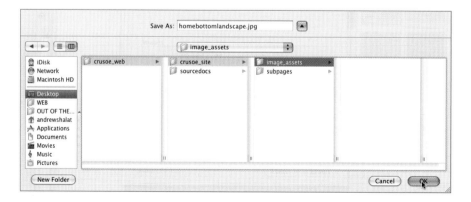

Before we close out of iPhoto, let's export our logo to the same folder. If your logo JPEG is larger than 175 pixels wide, you'll want to resize it down to 150 pixels wide before you export. Name the file logo.jpg, and send it to the image_assets folder.

You can quit iPhoto now and open AppleWorks. Choose a Word Processing document.

This isn't an HTML instruction book, and we're not going to make it one. But we are going to have to face the HTML beast at some point. Rather than have you learn your HTML, however, we'll step blindly into Web-page building on a basic level, and after we have a simple home page, we'll see what kind of code we've made without even knowing it. AppleWorks is astoundingly inadequate as a Web production tool, but it's pretty much the only thing we have at this point. So let's see how far we can get.

In terms of design, one of the most important components of a Web page is the HTML table. A table is the Web designer's building framework: By placing images and text in the cells of a table (often an "invisible" one, without ruled cell borders), you can impose order on free-flowing HTML content. Table cells can anchor graphics and give shape to text that would otherwise flow formlessly across the full width of a page. Table cells can determine where text blocks begin, how they align to the edges of a page or column, and how far they extend down and across a column or page. Empty table cells can be used to create margins and stake out white space between page elements. You can also use table cells graphically, assigning them different background colors or, with a bit of code tweaking, even different image backgrounds. In more sophisticated designs, you can nest tables, have tables within tables, and even layer tables on top of one another. Suffice it to say, the table is crucial to Web design.

With tables, we can do almost anything. but to take advantage of them, we need either a text editor (and some HTML coding skill) or a Web-design program that makes it easy to build and edit tables. And that's where the air escapes from our tires. Table handling in AppleWorks is rudimentary, and exporting an AppleWorks table to an HTML page can be likened to painting a portrait with one eye covered and your hands tied together with itchy horsehair rope in a dim room where the light flickers whenever you try to rise from the lumpy chair that your ankles are strapped to. In other words, we're not going to get a Gauguin from our efforts.

In AppleWorks, choose Table > Insert Table (Command+Y). Take a look at the preliminary sketch of the home page. If you were to break down the page into zones, you would have the top, with the logo and text, the navigation, and the bottom image. So let's try making this table three rows deep and one column across.

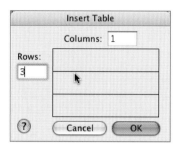

The cursor is now blinking in the topmost row, yes? If not, place your cursor so that it is. Choose File > Insert, navigate to the image_assets folder, and choose logo.jpg. (If the filename is grayed out, make sure to change the File Format in the Open: AppleWorks dialog box to All Available.) Click Insert, and your logo will appear where your cursor was blinking.

Now put your cursor in the middle table cell. Here's where we'll place our navigation. Remember, this is a very, very simple homepage. Type this text:

About Us | Contact | Gallery

Give the text a center alignment.

Now put your cursor in the bottom table cell. Insert the bottom image (choose File > Insert, navigate to image_assets, and choose homebottomlandscape.jpg).

Almost there. Take a look at your page.

We still need to put the name and some text in the top-right corner. Note that this isn't exactly like our sketch. Compromise, remember?

Put your cursor in the top cell. Choose Table > Select Current Cell; then choose Table > Subdivide Cells (Command+J). Change the cell from one column to two columns. Now, in the newly created top-right cell, we can type some useful information.

Referring to our business cards, type this text:

> Crusoe Deserted Island Tours
>
> 3rd Coconut Tree from the Beach
>
> Desert Island, South Seas

Let's stylize the text. Remember, however, that we really can't do much in terms of font selection, because we can't guarantee that any viewer will be able to see anything more sophisticated than serif, sans serif, normal, bold, or italic. So with that in mind, we'll make this easy. Format the font as Verdana 12 point. Then select the first line and style it bold.

The next two lines should be smaller. Make them 9 point.

Now put your cursor in the top-left cell. Use the text-alignment tool (located just above your ruler), and make the alignment Center. The logo will shift over to the center of the cell.

Open the Accents palette (Window > Show Accents, or Command+K). Put your cursor over one of the table's inner borders, and click. You'll know you have the border selected because it becomes a dashed line with the dashes moving (also known in some circles as "marching ants"). With the line selected, go to the Accents palette, select Pen, and choose Line Width "None". The border should disappear. Repeat this process for as many of the inner borders as you like. Although the lines will disappear while we're in AppleWorks, when we look at the page in a browser such as Safari, we'll still see borders on the table cells. But this elimination of lines will come in handy later on in the book.

Let's preview our file in a browser. Choose File > Save As (Command+ Shift+S) ,and in the ensuing dialog box, give the file a name such as preview.html. Then choose HTML from the File Format drop-down menu. Save the file to the Desktop for now so that it won't get us confused later when we're ready to save our final page.

Open Safari from your Dock. Choose File > Open File (Command+ O), and locate preview.html on the Desktop.

The page will open in Safari. Note that even though we chose Verdana, a sans- serif font, for our text style, the text is a serif font, most probably Times Roman.

Compromise.

Here's an experiment you may want to try. Choose Safari > Preferences > Appearance. Where it says Standard font, change the font to Verdana 16. Simultaneously look at your page in the browser. It will change to Verdana. How about that? This experiment should help emphasize to you how you have very little control—at this level, at least—of what people could do to the way they view your pages.

If you want type to stay as you intend it to, the fastest way to do so is to make it a graphic. But then you lose the ability as a viewer to copy the text as text to paste it somewhere else. Yet another compromise.

OK, back to AppleWorks.

In the second table row, we have our navigation line. Select the words About Us. In the toolbar above the page, click the Internet Link tool (two chain links over a globe). Here's where it gets a little tricky. We won't be putting a full-on http:// Web address here. There's no need, because our About Us page will be living in the folder we set up earlier, called sub-pages. So we'll need to write the *path* that will take a link there.

In the URL text area, type this text:

> subpages/aboutus.html

The *subpages* represents the folder, and the slash means within that folder, find *aboutus.html*, which is the page we're looking for.

We haven't even created the aboutus.html page yet. But because we have planned, at the very least, our file-folder architecture, we know where it *will* live as soon as we get around to making it.

Back on the page, select Contact. Click the Internet Link tool again. This time, we're going to make an email link. When the viewer clicks this link, his email application will automatically open, preaddressed with our email address.

In the URL text area, type this text:

mailto:stranded1@mac.com

(You can use your own email address.) Be sure not to use any spaces or uppercase characters. You can test this immediately in AppleWorks. Put your cursor over the contact link, and click. Voilà. Mail opens automatically.

That's a neat thing, but sometimes, it's nice to preassign the Subject line in the email message too. Easily done. Carefully select the Contact link without clicking it. Or before you do, click the icon just to the right of the Internet Link tool in the toolbar. This tool deactivates the links you make so that you can get your work done without inadvertently triggering links every two seconds.

With Contact selected, click the Internet Link tool again. The URL text area will be blank. Type your email address again, like this:

mailto:stranded1@mac.com?subject=Information Please

Note that after the equal sign, you don't have to abide by the lowercase, no-space rule.

Now activate the link by clicking the link activation/deactivation icon again, and click your Contact link. Your email application will open, but this time, the Subject line is already filled in.

Before we go on to link to the Gallery page, let's save this file. Now the native form of this page is not HTML, but AppleWorks. That means this is a *source* file, not a *processed* file. So we'll save it in the appropriate folder:

[Home]/Desktop/crusoe_web/sourcedocs

Are you beginning to see how the navigation system we use on the Macintosh is similar to the way we navigate links on the Internet?

Save your file as crusoehomesource.cwk in AppleWorks format. Please make sure that the file format is AppleWorks this time. Whew. Now we have a source document.

Let's make a gallery of images that we can link to from our home page.

Open iPhoto again.

For the sake of speed, we'll use just the six or seven images that we put in the Crusoe iPhoto album.

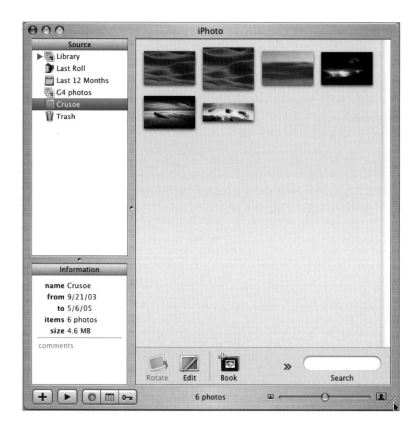

You may want to add or delete some of the images. As long as you have five or more, we're OK for this exercise. Choose View > Titles (Command+Shift+T) so that you can see the names of each image.

With just the album selected (Crusoe), choose Share > Export (Command+Shift+E). This time around, select Web Page in the Export Photos window. The title of the page will be prefilled with the name of your album—in this case, Crusoe. Type the title **Crusoe Gallery** for the sake of consistency with our Web site.

The default three columns, ten rows will work fine here. Notice that we can change the background color of the page, or we can fill it with a repeating or tiling image. Though these options might be appropriate for another site at another time, right now we're going for the simplicity we achieved on our page thus far.

We do, however, want to have the title of each image show up. If this were a commercial venture, we could add comments and be explicit about each image.

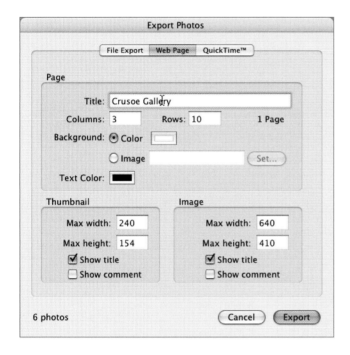

Now comes the crucial part. The pages we're about to create automatically will take their name from the folder we put them in. So we'll take our time when we navigate to our destination. Find your way to

Crusoe_web/crusoe_site/subpages

But don't click OK yet! On the left side of your Export Photos window, click the New Folder button. Name this folder gallery. Now you may click OK.

Open Safari, choose File > Open File (Command+O), and navigate to gallery folder you just created. The folder is now populated with three sub-folders and an HTML document named gallery.html. Select gallery.html.

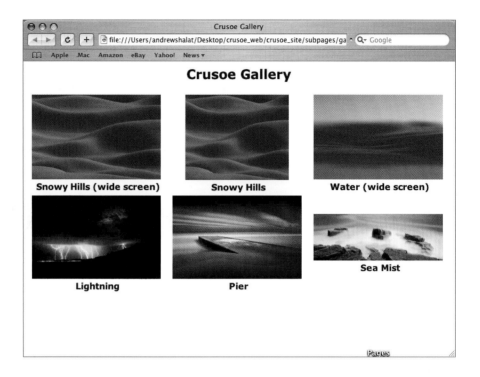

Now we know we have a gallery, so we can go back to our source document for the home page and link to it.

In AppleWorks, in crusoehomesource.cwk, select Gallery. Click the Internet Link tool. Now we have to remember how to get to the Gallery page.

For those of us with short-term-memory problems, here is the path:

subpages/gallery/gallery.html

For the sake of argument, we can say that this home page is almost done. There are just a few more steps left to complete it. Choose File > Save As, and put the file not in the sourcedocs folder, but in crusoe_site. Before you save it, rename it index.html. Now remember to save it in the correct format (HTML).

Test the file from within Safari. Find crusoe_site/index.html.

When it opens, test your Gallery link as well. Does it work? Good.

We have a few more steps in this process. We have to build our About Us page.

Open crusoehomesource.cwk, and save it as aboutus.cwk in the source-docs folder. Now we have two separate source documents, one for the home page and another for the About Us page.

Select the address text from 3rd Coconut Tree on down, and delete it. Press return and then type some biographical information.

The only thing we need to do is give visitors a way back to the home page. So delete the About Us link in the navigation text, and type **Home | About Us**. We want the About Us to remain in the navigation for the sake of consistency; we deleted it to get rid of the link, because the page doesn't need a link to itself. The normal text in the navigation will give a visual cue to the fact that you're now on *that* page.

Select the Home text. Using the Internet Link tool, type this text:

../index.html

The two dots and then the slash mean "Go up one folder level and find this page."

Save the page as aboutus.html in the subpages folder.

Open your home page in Safari. Test your links. The only problem with this site's navigation is the missing return buttons from the Gallery page. But we'll not bother with that now for several reasons, among which are our limited HTML editing tools. There are points in design when you just have to take your fingers off your keyboard, lift your hand from the mouse, and be satisfied with what you have. It's called…compromise.

Got a Web Page...Now What to Do with It?

●●●●●●●

Having a Web page on your local computer is a digital form of "all dressed up and nowhere to go." You can't just invite everyone over to your house to see the page. That sort of misses the point. And where would they all sit? The piano in the corner takes up too much room.

Up till now, we've been designing and producing work within the walls of Fortress Macintosh. But it's time to leave the nest *(piling metaphor on top of analogy).* The World Wide Web beckons, and your Macintosh sits poised to send you out into it.

We're making only one huge assumption in this section: that we all have an Internet connection. Unlike our time on the proverbial deserted island, back here in civilization, we are pretty much required to have connection to the Internet. Whether via cable, DSL, satellite or dial-up, we need to have our Macintosh connected to the Web. We would *prefer* (there's that word again) a high-speed connection, but that isn't essential if all we're doing is sending our files to the Web. A slower connection just means we'll spend a little more of our precious time watching progress bars.

When we first took our Macintosh out of the box, plugged it in, and turned it on, we were greeted with, among other things, an invitation to set up a .Mac (pronounced "dot-mac") account. Whether we accepted that kind offer back then didn't matter much. But now we are looking for a place to make our Web presence, and a .Mac account solves several key issues for us.

> TIP: YOU MAY NOTICE AT THIS JUNCTURE THAT WE HAVEN'T EVEN REACHED OUR "FOR A FEW BUCKS MORE" SECTION, AND WE'RE TALKING ABOUT A SERVICE THAT COULD OSTENSIBLY COST US A FEW BUCKS MORE. BUT WE GET AROUND THAT LITTLE BUGABOO BY EMPLOYING APPLE'S 60-DAY FREE TRIAL ON .MAC ACCOUNTS (DESCRIBED AT WWW.MAC.COM). WE'RE VERY CLEVER, WE MAC GUERILLAS, WE ARE.

A .Mac account will give us an email address. It will also give us online storage, a public area where we can share files with others, a Web address for our Web pages, and even a collection of predesigned Web pages we can fill with our own content. We'll get into the predesigned Web pages later in this chapter. But for now, let's see how we can get our homemade site online.

To establish a temporary (or long-term) .Mac account, or to visit one you've already set up, steer Safari to www.mac.com. Follow the instructions on creating an account, if necessary, and sign in using your account ID and password. When you're inside, click the HomePage link in the .Mac tab. We're going to avoid the prebuilt templates for the time being; instead, we simply want to establish a home for our test site. In the left pane, you will see a folder with your account name. Below that are Add/Delete/Edit buttons.

If you click the Add button, you can create a folder for your site. Keep an eye on the line above the column view that states "This site's address is," because that is the URL or Web address where you'll find your site. Name your new folder something like homemade_site. This way, we can look back on it someday and laugh. (Trust me—someday, we will.)

With the folder established, we can back out of .Mac and return to our Desktop. In the Finder, there is a Go menu. In the Go menu, you will see iDisk and an arrow to the right of it.

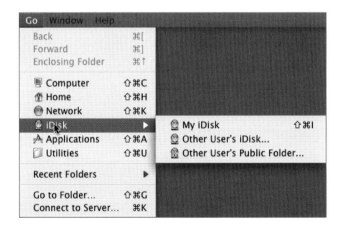

Choose Go > iDisk > My iDisk (Command+Shift+I). An iDisk icon, labeled with your account name, will appear on your Desktop. Open the iDisk, and you will see several folders. Find and open the Sites folder. Inside the

Sites folder, you will find the homemade_site folder you just created in .Mac. Here's a simple way of putting your homemade site on the Web: Drag the crusoe_site folder from your Desktop into the homemade_site folder on your iDisk.

Open Safari, and type this URL:

http://homepage.mac.com/*youraccountname*/homemade_site/crusoe_site

Now stare with mouth agape at your simple efforts, now published on the World Wide Web for all to see and appreciate (or criticize and judge).

That's one way to get on the Web. Now let's talk about the easy way. Because we've established a .Mac account, we can take advantage of the service's built-in Web-page design templates.

Log back in to your .Mac account, and go to HomePage. Below the column view is the Create a Page panel. The tabs to the left describe the various types of Web-page designs you can use.

Take your time wandering through all the different templates. When you're fully overloaded with the choices, have a drink of tea, clear your head, and relax. When you're completely rested, click the Writing tab.

Just for exploration's sake, click Archival. You're presented with a template and fill-in-the-blank areas. In the image area on the left is a Choose button that lets you fill that space with any image file in your iDisk's Pictures folder. Unless you've already placed some files in that folder, your choices at this point will be nonexistent, but we can remedy that:

Go back to your Dock, and open iPhoto. Select a few images from your library. Choose Share > Export. Choose File Export, JPG format, full-size images, and Use Album Name and Extension. Now click Export.

Because your iDisk is already open, you'll have the option of uploading these images directly to your .Mac account. Navigate to iDisk/Pictures, and click OK.

When the export is finished, return to Safari. Go back to the Archival template, and click Choose on the image box. Navigate to the Pictures folder, and find in your newly populated folder the image of your choice. Remember, it's important not to be random in your choices. Although I don't want to prescribe every aspect of your design, I strongly suggest that you choose an image that relates to our island theme, just to keep things consistent and your eye on the ball, as it were.

Inserting text is obvious. Fill the template with text from our original flier. Or insert this block of text (more about it later); see page 137:

> Lorem ipsum dolor sit amet, consectetuer adipiscing elit, sed diam nonummy nibh euismod tincidunt ut laoreet dolore magna aliquam erat volutpat.

When you use that text, you're joining in a 500-year-old tradition.

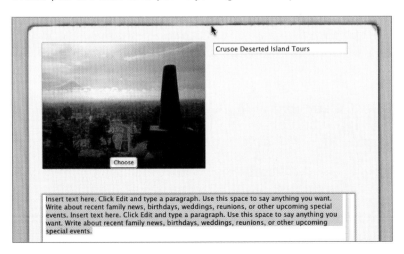

When you finish filling in the blanks, as it were, you can preview your page or just go right ahead and publish it. This is Web design made ultra-simple.

But a more interesting trick would be to use your Web page, courtesy of your .Mac template, in other media by taking a screen grab of it and keeping it as an image. Who knows? Maybe you will want to include it in a video in the future.

Let's go back to iPhoto for a moment. We still haven't fully exploited its sharing and instant Web-page facilities. Choose your Crusoe album. Choose Share > HomePage, or just click the HomePage icon in the toolbar at the bottom.

iPhoto automatically connects to your .Mac account and opens a window with your images placed in a template. You can change the template on the fly, using the template drawer sticking out of either the right or left side of the Publish HomePage window.

A Digression Concerning Counters

BE WARY OF USING COUNTERS. A COUNTER ON A WEB PAGE IS A DOUBLE-EDGED SWORD. LET'S CONSIDER THE REASON FOR PUTTING A COUNTER ON YOUR PAGE. IS IT FOR INFORMATIONAL PURPOSES, SO THAT YOU CAN KEEP TABS ON HOW MANY PEOPLE ARE VISITING YOUR SITE? IF SO, WHY LET EVERYONE ELSE KNOW THAT TOO? THERE ARE OTHER WAYS OF GETTING A LOG OF VISITS THAT DOESN'T AIR YOUR LAUNDRY IN PUBLIC.

WHAT IF YOU HAVE A SLOW WEEK? THERE ARE FEW THINGS SADDER THAN A LONELY WEB SITE THAT EVERYONE KNOWS IS LONELY. EVEN IF YOU SOMEHOW START THE NUMBERS ON THE COUNTER AT 23965, THE RATE OF INCREASE MIGHT NOT BE AS QUICK AS YOU WOULD LIKE. YOU RUN THE RISK OF HAVING VIEWERS THINKING THAT THEY'VE ALREADY MISSED THE BEST PART. AFTER ALL, NO ONE WANTS TO BE THE LAST ONE IN LINE. AND ONCE AGAIN, YOU FALL VICTIM TO LOOKING VERY UNPOPULAR.

LAWYERS ARE TAUGHT NEVER TO ASK A QUESTION IN COURT TO WHICH THEY DON'T ALREADY KNOW THE ANSWER. IN THE SAME VEIN, A COUNTER ON A WEB SITE IS A QUESTION WHOSE ANSWER IS UNKNOWN. SO IF YOU ASK THIS WEB DESIGNER TO PUT A COUNTER ON HIS SITE, YOU'D BEST BE PREPARED FOR REJECTION.

At the bottom are several options for the page. Most important just now is the Publish To drop-down menu, with which you'll choose the folder where your image gallery page will live. Buttons here let you choose whether your page will contain two or three columns, and check boxes let you specify whether the page should contain a Send Me a Message link and/or a counter that tracks the number of times the page is viewed.

iPhoto's connection to .Mac and your iDisk makes easy work of publishing photos.

Stealing From the Web

It's been said that "thieves copy, but artists steal." But as we discussed earlier in this book, a designer is not necessarily an artist, and as long as we don't get caught, we're not obligated to be either. So because we're neither of those two things—at least not, in this instance—we don't want to copy or steal. Maybe *borrow* is a better term. And who better to borrow from than ourselves?

If, after we set up a Web site using .Mac templates or themes and our own images, text, and tweaks, we should be able to reuse those layouts for other purposes, shouldn't we? If we can take screen grabs of our own pages or just portions of them, we might be able to incorporate them into PDFs for use in print materials about our site.

What, you say? Use print to spread the word about a Web site? Just because we're online doesn't mean we should abandon more traditional media, such as print. After all, we spent many hours earlier in this book carving out a flier and business cards. Using screen shots of our own site in promotional materials certainly qualifies as fair use.

In addition, it's OK if the .Mac templates inspire us to liven up our fliers or suggest new color schemes, textures, or layouts. Feel free to experiment with screen grabs; crops; and even iPhoto adjustments to color, hue, and saturation adjustments. Play around. Mix and match elements from .Mac (and Pages, Keynote, and even AppleWorks), and learn from the pros.

Concerning images on the Web that don't belong to us…well, my name isn't Picasso, Stravinsky, or even Monk, and I don't have the proceeds from multiple masterpieces to bankroll a copyright-violation defense.

More important, we as creative professionals (and even as creative neo-phytes) should recognize and respect the intellectual property of others, the way we'd expect others to respect the fruits of our labors. Digital technology makes it extremely easy to poach others' work, but the means don't justify the ends. Swiping ideas is a great way to learn, but swiping copyrighted images is just plain theft.

For a few bucks more

We've already covered the idea of opening a .Mac account. We can openly declare now that for a few bucks more, we can actually *pay for* the .Mac account and have full access to it for a full year, after which we can decide whether it still suits our needs.

And the odds are good that we all have, if not our own digital camera, access to one. With just a digital camera, a USB cable, and iPhoto, we have an escape tunnel into the wide, wide world. With a connection to the Internet, we have a breach in the wall of our fortress that goes beyond the wide world and enters into the realm of the imaginations of those who people the wide world.

Add a Scanner or Camera to the Mix

Let's start with a quick overview of how we can use a digital camera to enhance our use of images, fulfill our creative intentions, and get closer to that preferred state of things that we have been crawling toward this whole chapter.

Back in the days before the digital camera conquered the world, desktop scanners were the resource for designers seeking incidental graphic images. Getting photos into the Mac for use in digital design work was incredibly valuable. But with a little ingenuity, the scanner could do much more than that.

Need a stock graphic that says something about children? Arrange a few crayons on the scanner, and scan them into your favorite image-editing program. Want an intriguing background for a personal-finance piece? Spread some coins or bills around the scanner bed.

In creative hands, a scanner permitted easy acquisition of interesting textures, served as a collage and pattern-design studio, and even stood in as a quick-and-dirty still-life camera by capturing images of 3-D objects placed on the scan bed. And guess what? Scanners can still serve all those functions, and capable desktop scanners are so affordable that there's practically no excuse not to have one on your desk. (My first flatbed, a single-pass 24-bit scanner, ran a cool $2,000. You can get a better-equipped one for around $79 today.)

That said, the digital cameras so many of us carry in our pockets free the image- and texture-grabbing potential of the scanner from a desktop tether. With even a midrange camera, it's possible to find raw material for high-quality graphics anywhere and incorporate them into our designs in minutes.

Let's not use our digital camera just for family photos and shots of buildings. *Incidental* graphics often make for more interesting pages. If you have access to a digital camera, follow along with this exercise to see what we mean.

If your camera has a macro function, you can focus on objects very near the camera lens—sometimes less than an inch away. If your camera has this feature, turn it on, and grab an object with interesting surface textures—a dart, say, or your watch. Place it on a neutral, solid-color background (a blank piece of paper will do fine), and snap away from multiple angles.

If your camera has a macro feature (and even if it doesn't), coins are great for closeups. Take a penny out of your pocket, or find an old buffalo nickel, and get in close. Or if your camera needs greater distance, spread out an array of coins and shoot them.

Get as close to your subject(s) as you can without blurring the image, and take the shot. Then get closer. Remove the paper, crumple it up, and put it back. Try swapping different colors of paper or maybe aluminum foil. While you're in the kitchen, grab a bottle of olive oil, press the camera lens to the glass, and shoot through it. The distortions, refractions, and tints can be great raw material for background images, page borders, horizontal rules, and other graphic punctuation.

Let's try some more. Find a piece of fruit. Take a photo of an apple, a banana, and a grocery-store produce section. Take a collection of images. Do full master shots and then get up close. We'll use these images in the next exercise—a Web site for a possible Crusoe side business. Very hush-hush.

When you've harvested your produce images, connect your camera to your Mac. When you turn your camera on, iPhoto should automatically open and ask you to import your images. If this applies to you, you probably already know it, but some cameras must be in "image viewer" mode (as opposed to "take pictures" mode) to trigger an iPhoto import.

Import the images into iPhoto, and place them in a new album named Island Fruit. Now we're ready to do more Web development.

Use Keynote to Make Flash
●●●●●●●

For Web-site development, there *are* several high-end programs available. Macromedia Dreamweaver, Adobe GoLive, and Softpress Freeway are all excellent full-featured applications. Each works on both novice and expert levels. Bare Bones Software's BBEdit has long been considered the standard for Mac Web designers who prefer code-crunching to graphical authoring tools (and its freeware sibling, TextWrangler, is a great place to start your own experiments in HTML). Each of those programs mentioned deserves and has already its own instructional book.

If we look right in front of our own noses, however, we can find some interesting solutions for Web design and development. iWork contains two applications: Keynote and Pages. We've already worked in Pages, in Chapter 1. The interesting thing here is that whereas Pages will actually export a document as a Web page (HTML), most of the Pages templates are for print documents. By contrast, Keynote, which features many templates well suited to use on the Web, cannot generate HTML files. Keynote will, however, let you export files in a variety of Web-friendly

formats, including QuickTime, Microsoft PowerPoint, PDF, and Macromedia Flash.

Is there a way we can bridge these two programs to simplify Web-page
creation? Might we design a layout in Keynote, bring it into Pages, and
output the results to HTML? Well, not really. Pages' export to HTML
function is deceiving. Even if you take a template from Pages and export
it *as is* to HTML, you'll get *unexpected* results. We'll do an exercise in
Pages to exhibit this.

And even though we won't get a perfect Web page, we will learn a few
things along the way that will undoubtedly come in handy in other circumstances. Among other things, we will learn how to make our own template
and, in a pinch, export a file as a graphic into something we can put on
the Web.

But before all that, however, isn't there *something* we can do to produce a
Web page from iWork? Yes, there is. We'll take a closer look at Keynote's
export functions and support for a technology you've probably experienced as a Web surfer: the animation technology known as Flash.

Because Keynote is a presentation-production application, much of the
power and fun of using the program involve its transition features—which
enable animation of any and all objects on a page, individually or together,
and also enable animated shifts between slides. Exporting to Flash lets us
take those animated effects from the boardroom to the Web.

As we prep our Flash file in Keynote, we'll once again be employing a
source document/processed document methodology. The source document is the native Keynote file, and the processed document is the
Flash file.

Open Keynote to begin. As in Pages, you are first presented with a choice
of themes, or templates. Scroll through, and you'll notice that we weren't
kidding about the aspect-ratio format. These themes really do seem ready
for the Web—more than those we find in Pages.

Keynote is very similar to Pages. Both iWork applications use similar drag-
and-drop interfaces. Both use the Inspector palette to reveal and manipulate object attributes and behaviors. Even their color schemes and effects
are identical.

But look closely at the theme choice. At the bottom, you should see a Slide Size drop down menu. You have two choices: 800 x 600 and 1024 x 768. We recognize these options as pixel dimensions. At least they're talking in the right language. Make sure to keep 800 x 600 selected.

If we're going to follow along with our deserted-island styling, let's choose Watercolor for our theme.

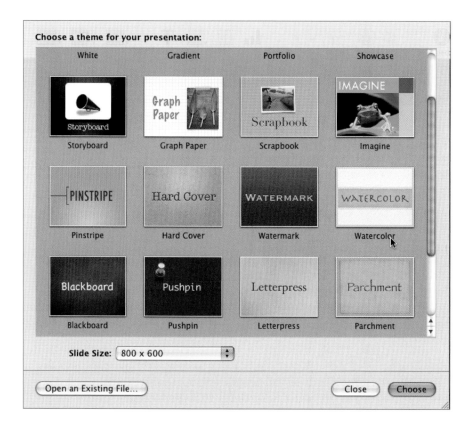

Your document will open in the theme you've chosen. By default, you should be in Navigator view. You can change that by clicking the View icon. At one point, we will be looking at Slide Only, but for now, let's just go all the way down in the View pull-down menu and choose Show Rulers.

Now go back to the top, and look at Masters. These are examples of the page-design variants within this theme. Let's make a design decision. Select a different master from the one we're now using. Go down to Title, Bullets & Photo, and select it.

Notice that your original layout just changed. Remember, this is going to be some kind of Web page, not a slide presentation, so this layout will act as our home page. In the bottom-left section of the window, you have your zoom options. Zoom out to 75 percent.

Put your cursor in the top Double Click to Edit text box. Press the space-bar. The text will disappear. Type **Island Fruits and Vegetables**. You may have to resize the text to fit. Choose Format > Font > Show Fonts (Command+T).

Start the same process in the left text box. Press the spacebar, and the text disappears. Now, instead of typing just one line, let's put a whole bunch of dummy text (to help speed the process along).

We'll fill this in with Latin dummy text—what we'll call *Lorem Ipsum* for short. Here's how to find some. Open Safari, and in Google, search for Lorem Ipsum. On the result page, choose one of the many Lorem Ipsum generator links.

Find a sample of the text, and copy it to your clipboard.

NOTE: WHEN YOU USE LOREM IPSUM, YOU SHOULD TAKE A MOMENT TO REALIZE THAT YOU ARE CONTINUING A TRADITION THAT HAS BEEN AROUND SINCE THE 16TH CENTURY. SINCE THE 1500S AND THE INVENTION OF MOVEABLE TYPE, PRINTERS AND TYPESETTERS HAVE BEEN USING THIS TEXT FOR FILLER. OK, ENOUGH DAYDREAMING ABOUT HISTORY. BACK TO WORK.

Paste your Lorem Ipsum into the new text area. Style the text so that it all fits within the text area without any overrun.

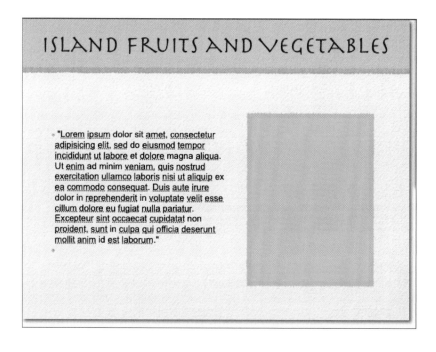

Open iPhoto. If you were listening earlier and have access to a digital camera, your Island Fruit album is ripe for the picking. If that's not the case, grab a camera and run—don't walk—to your fridge's crisper drawer.

In iPhoto, crop one of the images of fruit to match (basically) the rectangular shape on your Keynote layout. If you're unsure of the shape or just want to be more precise, go back into Keynote, make sure your rulers are in pixels, and drag guidelines around the shape. You do this by positioning your mouse over either the horizontal or vertical ruler, where the cursor will become a double line with arrows, and dragging into your live page. The ensuing guides will also tell you where you are on the page.

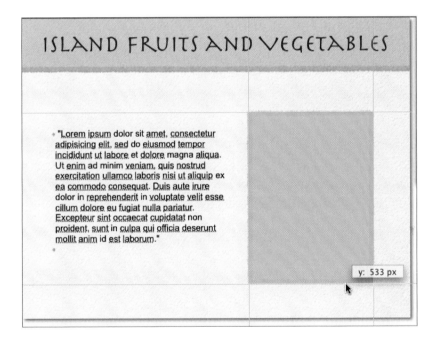

This will help you see the exact measurements for the image space you're trying to fit.

Another way to accomplish this is to grab a rectangle from the Shapes menu and simply drag it over the shape. As you resize the shape, you'll see a yellow tag that tells you its exact measurements.

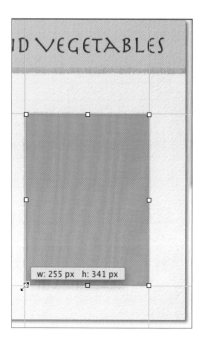

We have 255 x 341 pixels or thereabouts. Let's go back to iPhoto, where we can try our best to make our image that size.

In iPhoto's library, click your image, and bring up the Edit window. Next to the Crop tool is the Constrain pop-up menu. Select Custom from the menu. Type the values **255 x 341**. If the image goes landscape instead of portrait, don't panic—we'll just rotate the image. Click Done.

Back in the preview window, select your cropped image, and drag it from iPhoto directly onto your Keynote page.

The image will undoubtedly be too large—massive, in fact. But you can resize it to fit. Grab one of the corner anchor points, and resize your fruits to fit the rectangle.

Now let's do something cool. Click the image, go to the Inspector (View > Show Inspector), and select the Graphic Inspector. Now give the image a stroke of 1 pixel. Next, apply a drop shadow. Be aware, however, that some Keynote users have noted that Keynote transparency effects vanish from slideshows exported as Flash; this causes drop shadows to be rendered as (generally ugly) grayscale solids or step gradients. The workaround would be to make a screen grab of the image you want with the drop shadow and drop it in an HTML page.

There. You have now made the first of your Flash pages. Remember, of course, that this works just fine in its native format as a slide presentation, too.

A Flash site should have more than just one page, so let's create another. First, make sure you are in Navigator view (View > Navigator). Click the plus sign that says New. A blank page based on the same master page you are working on will appear.

The page has the same familiar Double-Click to Edit boxes and the same rectangle. But because we've already seen this page layout, let's try a different one. Choose Photo Horizontal from the Masters pop-up menu.

Type in some nonsense like **Yes, we have no bananas**.

Now get the size for the rectangle. (Remember the shortcut: Draw a rectangle over the area, and read the measurements. Then delete the shape.)

Go back to iPhoto, choose a likely image, and crop it to those specs (382 x 284 pixels on *our* page). When you drag the image onto your secondary page, it won't sit on top of your page but will come in behind it, with the rectangle working as a mask. On our first page, we left the rectangular shape that we used for measurement in place, and it acted as a shield that kept our imported image on top of the page.

Here, we've gotten rid of that shield, and we're taking advantage of Keynote's fancy masking techniques. It's not crucial that we resize the image here to fit, as long as we take care *not* to let it bleed beyond the page borders. When we convert to Flash, you'll see why.

In the meantime, we'll make two more pages. The next should be a text page. Click New in the top toolbar. Now change the master to Blank. Click the Text tool. It puts a small text block in the middle of the page. Go back to your first page, and select and copy (Command C) the Lorem Ipsum. Now return to the third page; select the text in the new text block; and rather than just pasting, choose Edit > Paste and Match Style (Command+Option+Shift+V).

Your text is now in the same style that was the default for this template.

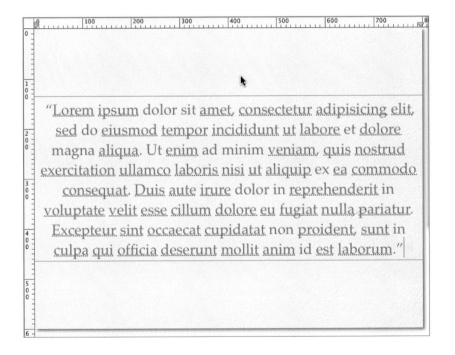

Good enough for government work. Make one more page. Choose Photo Vertical from the Masters pop-up menu. Type **Deserted Island Delicacies** in the top text box. In the lower text box, paste the Lorem Ipsum, matching the style. (You will have to cut out some of the dummy text to fit it all in.)

Now go back to iPhoto, choose a third image, and drag it to your page.

Making pages is, as you've seen, very easy. But we don't have any inter-activity yet. So let's go back to the first page. Click the Text tool. Drag the new text area to the area below the Lorem Ipsum. Select the text, leaving it in its original style, and choose Insert > Text Hyperlink > Email Message. Now look at your Inspector, which is displaying the Hyperlink Inspector. Fill in the pertinent information, such as your email address (or the address of the person to whom you'd like the email link to go) and the subject. Leave Contact in the Display area.

Back on the page, Option-drag the contact text to the right, and position it directly below your image. Change the text from Contact to Next. The text will be selected, so in the Inspector, change the Link pop-up menu from Email Message to Slide. Choose Next Slide.

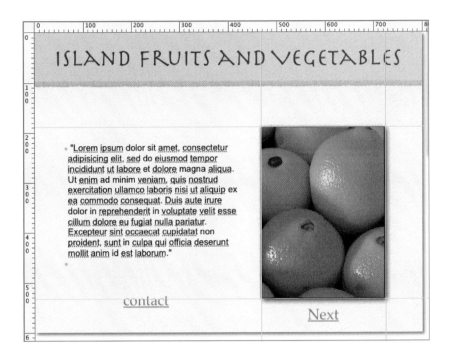

Go back to the page, select both Contact and Next, and copy them (Command+C).

Go to page 2, and paste (Command+V). Reposition the text so that Contact is centered under the existing text and Next is in the bottom-right corner. Create one more text link, and put it in the bottom-right corner. Type the text **Home**. Make it a slide link to First Slide. The text also gets a little return icon next to it. Now select the three text blocks, and copy and paste them on the following page.

Notice that the text always pastes in place. Paste the same three links on the final page.

Now let's put interesting but efficient transitions between the pages. (Note that we're still calling them *pages* rather than *slides,* keeping our focus on our design intention: a Flash Web site.)

In the Slides pane, select the first slide. In the Inspector, click the slide. Select the Transition pane. In the Effect section, choose a transition. Explore the options, but remember the Rule of Thumb to keep it simple.

It's a good idea not to scatter too many different transitions in your presentation. You want the transitions to *enhance,* not *distract.* We're choosing Dissolve and setting the duration at 0.50 second.

Now click the second slide in the Slides pane. Assign a transition to that slide as well. Continue this routine for each of your slides/pages.

Test your creation.

Before we commit to exporting this as a Flash document, let's save it in its native format.

Now click the Play button. Does it work? Of course it does. Is there anything missing? Well, let's see.

Let's go through the user interface and see what it needs.

It clicks forward fine. But you can't visit the previous page unless you go back to the home page and start over again. This is a fairly minor quirk, but a quirk nonetheless—one that we'll undoubtedly meet again in future projects.

Go back, on your own, and put the new link for Previous Slide on every page that requires it.

When you're finished with that, come back to this point in the book. I'll wait.

When you're ready, choose File > Export, and select Flash. Unclick the Hide Extension button in the Save window. Give your file a good name (lowercase, no spaces). The three-letter extension swf will follow automatically . Save your file.

Open Safari, locate your SWF file, and test it.

Refer to the first part of this chapter to send the file to your iDisk.

A Lesson in Frustration

Run through this exercise when you have an hour to spare and won't feel ripped off it you don't get the results you're hoping for. Remember, it's all about compromise. If you truly want to become a designer, you can experience firsthand the sense of angst and disgust that designers all too often experience in their routine. You may also learn some neat tips about how to create new templates, resize others, and see some of the limitations of Pages.

Be forewarned—Pages is not a Web-design program. But in the case of our exercises, it works great as a design and layout program, and we'll use it as such. It's exporting to HTML that gives us the bugaboo that has followed us along this whole trip: unexpected results.

Our process takes a layout that we like from Keynote and makes it a new template in Pages. Then we'll populate the template and export it as a PDF file. Using the PDF as a graphic, we'll import it into AppleWorks. We can add links in AppleWorks, if we like. From there, we can use our .Mac account with iDisk to upload the new Web page online.

Here we go.

Let's use the same layout we just used for our Keynote Flash pages. Open Keynote, and choose the Watercolor template. Select the Title, Bullets & Photo master.

Put your cursor in the top Double Click to Edit text box, and press the spacebar. The text will disappear. Do the same for the text box on the left.

Make a selective grab (Command+Shift+4), and grab the page, including the drop shadow. Try not to get the rulers in the picture.

Go out to your Desktop, find the picture you just made, and open it in Preview to make sure it's the one you want. Name the image keynote_layout1.

Close Keynote, and open Pages.

Choose the Blank template. Choose View > Show Layout so that you can see your rulers, header, footer, and central text box. The page is letter size by default, but that's way too big for our needs. Choose File > Page Setup

(Command+Shift+P). We want to limit the size of the page to around postcard size. You may already have a printer selected in the Format For menu. If so, look under Paper Size for 4″ x 6″ Postcard. Then orient the postcard to print landscape.

If your printer doesn't supply you that choice or something close to it, choose Any Printer from the Format For menu. If that Paper Size section doesn't have a 4″ x 6″ Postcard, click the Settings pop-up menu and select Custom Paper Size. Click New, give the paper size a name such as Postcard 6 x 4, and enter appropriate values in the Paper Size boxes. Make the Printer Margins .025 all the way around. Save your settings.

Back in Page Setup, choose Format for Any Printer, and in the Paper Size section, find your newly customized settings. Click OK.

Now you have a new paper size in Pages—not the easiest or most intu-itive way of going about it, but it gets done. Notice that the header, footer, and text box remain in the same relative positions in this layout as they were in the original.

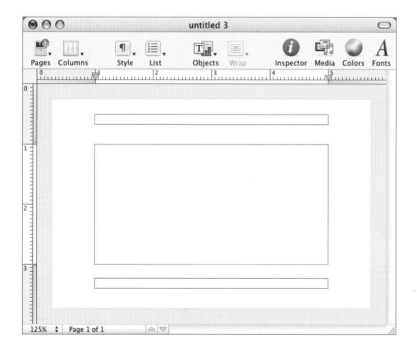

Now for the fun part. Go to your Desktop, and drag the screen-grab image we named keynote_layout1 onto your new postcard-size page. It probably will be way too big. That's OK. Open your window so that you can see all the anchor points defining its perimeter, grab the bottom-left one, and resize the image to fit on your page. It may get confusing with the layout guides and rulers, but after you have the image to size, choose View > Hide Layout (Command+Shift+L).

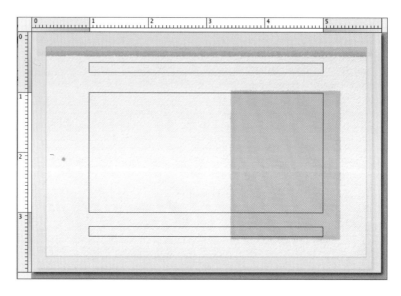

With the layout off, select the image. Choose Format > Advanced > Make
Master Objects Selectable. Next, choose Format > Advanced > Move
Object to Section Master.

The selection points on the Keynote grab disappear. That image is now
part of the master page in your new layout.

We must now define placeholders for text and graphics on our page.
Using the color spaces in our grab as guides, put a text box on the top.
Choose Objects > Text. Position the text box at the top.

We'll make this text part of the template we're building. Oh, you knew we
were building a new template, didn't you? It's a side benefit. That way, you
can always go back and do another.

In the text box, type **Island Fruits and Vegetables**. Now we get to define
a new type style as well. Because this is a Web template, remember,
we're extremely limited in what kind of fonts we can use. We call that
com-pro-…well, you know.

If you choose View > Show Styles Drawer, you'll see some basic, generic
paragraph styles. With your headline selected, click Heading in the Styles
Drawer.

Click the Fonts tool in the toolbar. Heading is probably defined as Helvetica 18 point; make it 24 point. You can change the color of the text as well, if you like—to something fruity, perhaps.

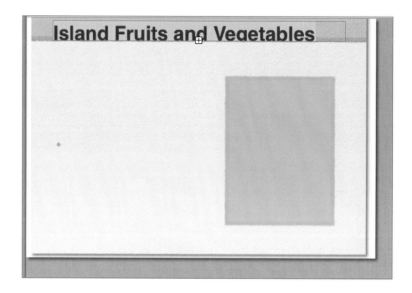

Now click the small plus sign at the bottom of the Styles Drawer. By default, it will be called Heading 2. Click OK.

Fit the text box so that all the text is completely visible. While the text is still selected, choose Format > Advanced > Define as Placeholder Text.

Next, go to iPhoto. If you went through the short digital-camera exercise earlier in the chapter, you should have a small collection of fruit and vegetable images.

In iPhoto, find a good closeup of a piece of fruit. If you feel that it needs to be cropped, double-click the image, and make the appropriate adjustments. Click and drag the image from iPhoto directly onto your page.

Resize the image so that it fits within the bounds of the rectangular shape on your page. Even if it doesn't fit perfectly to the same aspect ratio, that's OK. Position it so that it rests more in the top half than centered or lower.

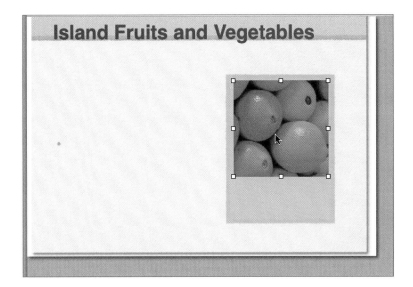

In the Graphic Inspector (Command+Option+I), give the image a drop shadow for dramatic effect. You may want to give it a stroke as well, to help it stand out. With the image still selected, choose Format > Advanced > Define as Image Placeholder.

Below the image placeholder (your fruit image), put a new text area. Type something to describe the image above it. From the Styles Drawer, apply the Caption style.

Select the caption text, and choose Format > Advanced > Define as Placeholder Text.

Once more, create a text area. This time, place it in the blank area to the left of our image. We'll fill this in with Latin dummy text, our Lorem Ipsum from the preceding exercise.

Paste the Lorem Ipsum into the new text area. Style the text with a serif font this time. Times 10 point will do.

Again, select the text, and define it as placeholder text (Format > Advanced > Define as Placeholder Text).

Now it's time to make this small page an official template. Follow closely. Choose File > Save as Template.

That's all. Now name the template. Remember to give it a name that reflects its purpose. How about homemadehomepage?

The file will be saved in the My Templates pane of the Template Chooser. But we're not limited to that location. If we like, we can always make a new rubric by creating a new folder in Library/Application/Support /iWork/Pages/Templates. The name of the new folder will show up in the Template Chooser as a new category.

Now you understand how to create new templates from scratch. You can also go through the same process using any of the existing templates already in Pages, as well resize them if necessary or modify them in any way you like.

But here's the bad news: Make any adjustments you like to the text and the images, but don't do too much work, because you'll be disappointed. Just give the page a new headline. Now export it as HTML. Give the page a distinct name.

Take a minute for yourself. Stretch your legs. Listen to iTunes. When you're ready, open Safari, and find your HTML file. Now you can yell. What the…?

Take a breath. It's all about compromise.

How do we remedy this? The old-fashioned way. Go back to Pages. Export your Pages file as PDF, insert it into AppleWorks, center the file on the page, and save as HTML. Before you do, you may want to add contact links or navigation.

Now open the page in Safari. It's a sort of dead file with one image. But you can send it to the Web, using your .Mac account and iDisk.

That's a lot of work for a little result. And you *want* to be a designer? Read on, dear supplicant.

Silver Lining

In case you haven't noticed, this isn't just a book about the Mac. The Mac is the best tool for a digital life, and there's no denying that. But remember, it's a tool. Of course, we are allowed—even encouraged—to fall in love with our tools. Our tools take on aspects of our personalities, and we take on portions of their peculiar features. But we're talking about issues that are universal to not just the Mac, or design; not just to Web design; not just to the beauty of the Macintosh itself (although that is a large part of what we're talking about). We're examining and proscribing aspects of language—design as a form of language. It's using signs and sounds and shapes to communicate a message across the gulf between one human and the rest of humanity. The frustration and dead ends we uncover during our design process are never useless.

Payoff is not always immediate. We took some wild turns in this exercise, and we cajoled and forced our ideas on the software. We did not, however, let it dictate to us. These are lessons that are the hardest to teach, but they are the most valuable. Never forget the ground we've covered here. In a different context, it will always work as an asset.

To Sum Up

You might feel as though you've been through the wringer after that last exercise. But ideally, it taught you some valuable lessons and skills that are not specific just to iWork. Among those lessons is the emphasis on being able to use what you can from diverse applications and combine them into a workable product.

Design on your Macintosh is something like cooking a great meal. You add different ingredients, sometimes unexpected ingredients, to make your dish. And it's not always the recipe that's written in the book that brings out the best flavors.

It's surprising that at this point, the Macintosh out of the box doesn't embrace direct Web-design functionality the way it handles print or, as we'll see in the next chapter, video and audio.

Because of this fact, it's important that we use all our wits to combine the basic skills such as making screen grabs, exporting as PDF, and taking still-life images of everyday objects such as fruits and vegetables to produce good design—or at the very least functional design.

Designing for the Web is a series of compromises and heartaches. Well, it's not really that bad. But the difference between that so-called preferred condition and the one you end up with can be great.

The best way to minimize that gulf is to invert your expectations from designer to user. Put yourself in the position of the user, not the designer. Walk through your design architecture, and see how much sense it actually does make.

Unless you're in the business of selling bells and whistles, don't use too many. Form and function do a little dance. Sometimes, the form will take the lead; other times, function does. Keeping this in mind will help you as you gather all your skills and hone your intentions.

That's enough pedantic proselytizing about design. Now let's go on to the real fun: video production *out of the box.*

Chapter Three: Video and Movies Out of the Box

3

I'd like to say that movies are easy. After all, all we really need for a movie are three elements: images, sound, and movement. Sounds easy, doesn't it? Well, with images, sound, and movement, we don't really have a film, though, do we? We have a slideshow. What else could it be that we're missing? (And don't say, "A ticket." Wisenheimer.)

Of course! The element we're missing is story. We can't forget about story. Without story, a movie is just a series of images and maybe some sound. So, to review, our chief tools for movie making number *four,* not three. To have a movie, we need images, sound, movement, and story.

Oops—one more thing, too. If you ever speak with directors, they'll inevitably tell you that all those four components are important, but they need one more thing: a point of view. Point of view, after all, is the one element that infuses every frame of our film. It is a movie's voice. It gives the movie its perspective, its context, and its end-point. It's invisible, like the air. In a way, point of view is the atmos-phere in which the film breathes. Or maybe it's like the yeast that makes dough rise.

  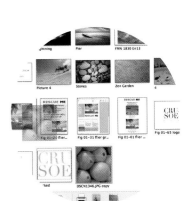

To those of you who are familiar with movie-making jargon, please don't confuse my references to point of view with literal camera-based point of view or the script direction *POV.* These terms refer to the use of the camera as a character's "eyes." I'm concerned with the theme of the movie. A director's point of view and a camera's point of view are two distinct things. Point of view is a *superconsideration* of message, audience. It is, in other words, the *creative intention* in the work. It may not even be obvious to us until we're deep in the creation process, which is why it's so hard to define beforehand.

More than any of the other design problems we've come across, from print to Web, making a movie *requires* a point of view. In print, you have the elements on the page working with one another and against one another, in contrast or in accord. The medium is flat and has no sense of time. It's nonlinear. You can pick it up at any point and absorb its meaning from different angles. With Web design, we're also working in a flat medium. You can click anywhere and go anywhere within a Web site at your whim, without a prescribed, linear, point A-to-point B map.

But movies have a linear progression. Remember, animation and movies need movement. And we measure our moviemaking as motion over time. The units we use are *frames per second.* This is no Buddhist malarkey, in which there is only a Now; this is brass-tacks stuff. There are a beginning, a middle, and an end. In the final work, your point of view may not be easily discernible to the casual viewer. It may not be apparent to you. But that's not important. What's important is to keep consistency in your message, keep your story clear in front of you, and give the piece a sense of unity and completeness.

Of the five essential ingredients for a movie—images, sound, movement, story, and point of view—the first three are readily accessible with what comes in the Macintosh box. And we won't have to go into a few bucks more, either—at least not until we get well beyond the fundamentals of storytelling and feel the need for special effects or advanced techniques such as compositing (layering scenes via blue or green screen).

The only things the Mac can't supply are story and point of view. We'll have to conjure those ourselves. We'll use the story we've all been carrying around in our imaginations for a while now—the tale of our castaway adventure—as source material. And we'll draw some inspiration from the Mac and the work we did in previous projects.

We'll use separate applications to create each of our basic ingredients: iPhoto for images, GarageBand for sound, and iMovie for movement. Our basic methodology will be much the same as it was in earlier projects. We use different tools to prepare elements of the project, solving specific design problems as we go, and then pull the various elements together in a broad layout, or *delivery* application.

We'll start with our images , iPhoto, and an exercise that will help us firm up our story even as we prep our files. We don't have to write a script per se, but we'll do what they do in film school: take 12 to 20 images and put them in an order that tells our story.

Next, we'll dive headfirst into one of the greatest breakthrough applications since support-hose socks for men. I'm talking about GarageBand, the music-composition and -creation software that lets us think we're musicians, even when we're not.

Finally, we'll bring everything together in iMovie HD.

Video Component 1: Images

In this exercise, we will make a 1- to 2-minute-long film. That may not sound like a long film, but if you think about it, most commercials are 30 seconds long, yet they convey whole stories within that short time frame.

Because we don't all necessarily own or have access to a digital video camera, we'll use still images only. But don't worry—we can achieve a semblance of movement with stills.

Our bigger challenge will be to collect 12 to 20 *significant* images that we can use as the building blocks of our movie. Our point of view, that ethereal but essential ingredient, will emerge through our design choices— which images we select and how we arrange and sequence them to tell our story.

Fortunately, in the course of preparing our print- and Web-design projects, we have acquired plenty of images that are appropriate for our movie . If you kept your files in order during the earlier exercises, you should have no trouble locating your various images and files from those exercises. Pick your favorites from among the final designs you made yourself—the postcard, logo, and business card, for example—and take screen grabs of them, cropping out duplicates from the postcard and business-card lay-outs as appropriate. Also, feel free to plunder the images you gathered as raw material for those projects, such as the screen-saver and Desktop images—those you used and those you didn't.

NOTE: NOW MAY BE THE APPROPRIATE TIME TO MENTION SPOTLIGHT, THE SEARCH TOOL IN MAC OS X 10.4 (TIGER). SPOTLIGHT, WHICH YOU'LL FIND EITHER BY CLICKING THE SMALL MAGNIFYING-GLASS ICON IN THE TOP-RIGHT CORNER OF YOUR SCREEN OR SIMPLY PRESSING COMMAND F, WILL ALLOW YOU TO FIND VIRTUALLY ANYTHING ON YOUR HARD DRIVE. UNLIKE PREVIOUS FIND FUNCTIONS, SPOTLIGHT LETS YOU FIND WORDS IN THE CONTENT OF FILES, RATHER THAN JUST THEIR FILENAMES. IT INDEXES YOUR HARD DRIVE IN THE BACKGROUND ALL THE TIME YOU HAVE YOUR COMPUTER TURNED ON, CONSTANTLY UPDATING DATA. AND IT'S A SUPERFAST WAY OF FINDING AND ACCESSING FILES. SO IF YOU'VE BEEN LESS THAN PERFECT AT KEEPING YOUR FILES IN ORDER, THE OPERATING SYSTEM CAN BAIL YOU OUT.

We've probably got a pretty hefty collection, but let's supplement it with a few images from the Web. We've already talked about the legal and ethical implications of using stuff you find online. Do the right thing, and download and use only images you have explicit permission to use.

Do a Google Images search for *shipwreck,* and find a suitable image you will have permission to use. If you have iPhoto 5, you can import images directly from Safari into your iPhoto library by Control-clicking an image and choosing Add Photo to iPhoto Library from the pop-up menu.

While we're surfing, don't forget the role the Mac played in our drama. Point your browser to www.apple.com, or do another Google search and grab an image of your Mac model.

When you've collected your source images, place them in the source images folder, open iPhoto, and import them (File > Add to Library or Command+O). Bring all the images into iPhoto. Place the images in an album, and pick the top 20 or so that you feel best evoke our castaway adventure—and the work it's inspired.

We're almost ready to start previsualizing our movie, but first, let's make one more graphic from scratch: a title card that will convey something of our story and help set the tone for the rest of our image choices.

Open TextEdit, and type this text:

> Island: from the Old English, *ïegland*, or watery land. Also, see the Latin, *Insula*.

(To get the double-dotted *ï*, press Option+U and then i.)

We'll design this as a placard, which will serve as the opening frame. But we should design the text first.

Bump up the size of the first word, *Island,* to give it emphasis. Then try shifting the colors of the other important words, *ïegland* and *Insula.* Remember to consider the delivery system, or medium, we're using. The layout is closer to Web design than to a paper flier. Make sure it's simple, readable, and large. If you prefer an exotic font (such as Papyrus or Herculanum), go for it. As long as it's not a distraction but works as an additive feature, it's OK. Remember: simplify, simplify, simplify.

Island:

from the Old English, *ïegland,* or watery land.

Also, see the Latin, *Insula.*

When you're satisfied with your design, take a selective grab, and save it to a new folder on your Desktop. You may want to name the folder something appropriate, such as Island_video. Now open iPhoto, and import that image. (File > Add to Library, or Command+O).

Make a new album, and name it storyboard (for reasons we'll explain momentarily). Drag all your collected images from the library into the album, and start weeding.

Our design decisions can make or break any project, and the most important decisions we'll make in our movie consist of our image choices. Our final set of about 20 images must tell our story of shipwreck, desertion, resourcefulness, and rescue. Our movie will ultimately use only 12 images, so there's more cutting to come, but we should always have more "footage" than we can use, to keep some options open.

Review the images in the album, keeping those storytelling elements in mind, and delete all but the 20 or so images that best represent those elements. Take your time. Don't rush.

Professional photographers and art directors, by nature of their business, must view and review thousands of images. To help make sense, process all the visual information, and make good design decisions, they often assign ratings and add commentary to images. In the predigital age, they would do this with wax pencils, but with iPhoto and other more high-end image-cataloging applications, we can simply type these annotations—and search for them later.

To do so, open iPhoto's Sources panel (the left album list), if it isn't open already; select an image in the main browser window; and click the *i* button in the bottom-left portion of the iPhoto window. Click in the information panel that appears in the bottom of the Sources column to add comments or apply a rating of one to five stars. If you merely want to rate an image, Control-click it in the browser window and choose a rating from the contextual menu.

Got your list of candidate images pared down? Your choices may differ from ours, but here's what we settled on for our final list:

Our Island-definition title card

Two beach shots from our flier exercise

Seven images from the Desktop Images collection (four of water and one each of beach rocks, shore rocks, and sand)

The shipwreck image we found in a Google search

One of the fruit-texture images that we used in our Web-design exercise

Five samples of our design work: three screen grabs of our flier, one of the Crusoe logo, and one of the business card

A Web image of a Mac (an iMac G5, in my case)

Storyboarding with iPhoto

Now that we have the "finalist" images in our album, we can sort through them, crop them if we must, change colors, and duplicate and edit them on a very basic level. But most important, we can begin arranging our images to tell our story and start to visualize our movie. In essence, we'll use iPhoto (and its slideshow function) as a *storyboarding* tool.

If you've ever watched one of those "Making of" features included with DVD bonus materials, you have probably heard of *storyboarding*. Those minidocumentaries almost always include a segment on the planning of the movie, in which the director mentions or refers to sketches of a particular scene or sequence. Those sketches are storyboards.

Storyboards are drawings or diagrams that represent each *shot,* or individual film sequence, in a movie or video. Storyboards are critical to the planning of the movie: Putting storyboards in order (and rearranging them and re-rearranging them) helps a filmmaker determine the best way to tell a story. On productions more elaborate than ours, they also help the director tell his or her fellow storytellers—the cast and crew—how each shot and scene will work.

We'll use iPhoto as a kind of storyboarding tool to help us get our ideas together. We'll use it to arrange our images, to get an idea of how best to tell our story.

Remember to use the text graphic we made, as well as the images of our fliers and logo. Our story arcs from shipwreck and exile, through struggle, inspiration, and triumph. Try to convey that through the arrangement of images.

Shift your images around the way you would when working on a tile puzzle. Try different sequences. Try Control-clicking just a few noncontiguous images, and make a slideshow out of them. Or make a second album, and use only a subset of your images to get a different perspective. (You can use iPhoto 5 to make multiple slideshows from a single album, but don't use that feature here; we'll need an album that corresponds exactly to your slideshow later on, when we switch to editing in iMovie.)

Images you delete from an album or slideshow are still saved in the iPhoto library, so don't worry about losing anything. You can come up with as many albums and slideshows as you like and review them at your leisure.

We started this exercise by creating a text graphic. Although that may have seemed like a title page, we actually want it to work in the same way that the images work: reinforcing the flow of the story. In other words, the text is less explanatory or expository than it is exemplary. We use it for dramatic effect, to show and give tone and voice, not to explain.

So we don't necessarily want that graphic to come first in the procession of images. Try ordering the images so that the story they tell is something like this: water > water > ship in storm > rocks > island > shore > beach > sand > food > Macintosh > fliers > logo > business card.

That's a story. That's a storyboard. Later we'll move on to the soundtrack. We'll be back for these images later, when we put them all together in iMovie.

When you've got a sequence you like, you can preview it by clicking the Slideshow button in iPhoto and then the Preview button (to view the slides inside the iPhoto window) or Play (to watch them in full-screen mode).

Our story sequence is set, but there are many more storytelling options to consider and more design decisions to make. But it's time to see your ideas in action. Go ahead and watch the show.

Refining our storytelling

If you want to tweak the sequence further, go ahead. When you're ready, we'll consider some additional refinements to our show.

Click the Settings button, toward the bottom–right corner of the slideshow window.

The Settings panel that appears controls some significant attributes of the slideshow (which will eventually become our movie), including how long each slide stays onscreen after it appears and how one slide will *transition* to the next.

Note that the settings here are global for the slideshow. You can adjust the settings for every slide individually (as we'll soon discuss). These default settings determine the behavior of slides you don't customize.

There's no need to change the standard settings now, but you can experiment with them to see how they affect the show. When you're finished, make sure that the automatic Ken Burns Effect option (available only in iPhoto 5) and the Repeat Slideshow boxes are unchecked.

Check out the options in the Transitions pull-down menu. The preview window shows you what each effect does, the slider lets you control the speed of some transitions, and the compass-point buttons let you choose the direction from which some of them are applied. (The slider and/or buttons are grayed out for settings that aren't adjustable.) We'll talk more about transitions in a moment, but when you're finished, leave the default transition setting for the slideshow at None and close the Settings panel.

From the Slideshow window, we can now customize the behavior of each slide (or scene in our movie) individually. Any settings you change from the controls in this window will apply only to the slide displayed in the main window. The Preview button lets you see the results of these slide-specific adjustments.

Use the forward and back arrows in the bottom-right corner to move from slide to slide. If you're using iPhoto 5, you can also switch slides by clicking one of the thumbnail images in the pane above the main window.

If you're not using iPhoto 5, you can skip ahead to the "Making a transition" section or stick around to hear about a cool feature that may make you want to upgrade: the effects setting Apple calls the Ken Burns Effect.

The Ken Burns Effect is named after the historical documentarian of PBS fame whose style of filmmaking often involves panning and zooming across still images while narrating. By moving from a closeup on one detail of a photo to another, or backing out from a tight focus on one subject to reveal others around it, Burns gets a sense of motion from still images. His techniques allow a single picture to tell a story with a beginning, middle, and end.

After you've played with the Ken Burns Effect a few times, it will become pretty easy to use: Activate it with the Ken Burns Effect check box, and control the effect using the zoom slider (in the bottom-right section of the iPhoto window) and the Start/End toggle. By default, Start view is selected first. Move the zoom slider to the right to pull in for a closeup, and click in the window to reposition the zoomed image with the hand tool. When you're done, switch the toggle to End, and you'll be back at a full view of the slide. If you do nothing further, your slide will appear in closeup view and back out to full-image view. If you set a new zoom level and position for End view, your slide will move to it from the closeup in Start view.

Note that the Ken Burns Effect moves from start to end at constant speed within whatever amount of time the affected slide appears onscreen. If you want to slow the effect, increase the slide's screen time in the Adjust panel.

We can apply the Ken Burns Effect to any or all of our images, but that doesn't mean we should. Some images don't warrant movement; others might need the slow reveal that this effect gives us. The Ken Burns Effect is a powerful tool, but we should use it only where it helps us tell our story more effectively. It's a design decision.

Making a transition

After we've placed and ordered some of images, if not all of them, and applied the Ken Burns Effect where needed, we must decide how best to move from each image to the next.

The simplest way to do this is to create what filmmakers call a *hard cut,* in which one image or shot ends and another appears. The alternative is a more elaborate *transition,* such as a dissolve or a wipe, in which a special effect is used to bridge shots or images. (Setting the default transition for our slideshow to None means our images are separated to begin with by hard cuts.)

Moviemakers typically use hard cuts between shots within a scene, as when the camera shifts between characters in a conversation. The audience is often not even consciously aware of them. Transition effects, on the other hand, call attention to themselves.

Individual transitions tell the audience something about the relationship between the scenes or images they connect. The relationship can be purely narrative—we've moved from one setting or set of characters to another—or thematic. A cross-fade or dissolve can show a change over time or connect one thought to another—a train of thought. A screen shimmer can alert us to a dream sequence or a flashback—an effect so familiar that it's often used these days for ironic or satirical effects.

Collectively, transitions affect the pacing, rhythm, and tone of the movie as a whole. They are more punctuation. They still help us tell our story and clarify our point of view. So you can see how the choices we make about transitions are important design decisions.

Selections from the Transition pull-down menu affect the move from the current slide to the next. If a transition's speed and direction can be tweaked, you'll find the controls in the Adjust panel.

As with the Ken Burns Effect, transitions can be effective storytelling tools, but that doesn't mean they're always needed. Before applying a transition between images (movie shots), let's take a moment and ask ourselves: Do we want to draw any special attention to our transition? And if so, why?

Experiment with transitions, and see how they affect the tone and pacing of our story. Change the screen time for the slides before and after the transition, and use the timing sliders to tweak the effect's speed. Don't be too fussy, because we won't add final transition effects until we're editing in iMovie, but get a sense of which transitions work for which scenes—and where they don't work at all.

Remember, simplicity is often best, and it can be hard to achieve—especially with all these gadgets and doohickeys at our fingertips. Choose wisely.

Making a preliminary movie

By using the options in the Share menu, we could declare our movie finished now and just convert our slideshow, with its transitions (and music, if you added any), directly into a QuickTime movie. To do so, select your slideshow in the Sources list, choose Share > Export, and select one of the three size options: small, medium, and large. The choices refer to both the size of the QuickTime window and the size of the file in megabytes. With 20 images, set Large, the final .mov file is around 60 MB. That's way too large for emailing or most Web applications, but it'll give you the best-quality preview of your movie, and it's probably the best choice for now, assuming that you have sufficient space on your Mac's hard disk.

Export the movie (at any size), and enjoy the fruits of your labors. This is only a rough draft of our final movie, but it's a good start. It also gives us an idea of the movie's duration, or *run time,* which will be an important consideration when we prepare our soundtrack. When you're done watching the movie, use the Finder's Get Info function on the movie file. Look in the More Info section for its duration, and make a note of it. We'll refer to it again.

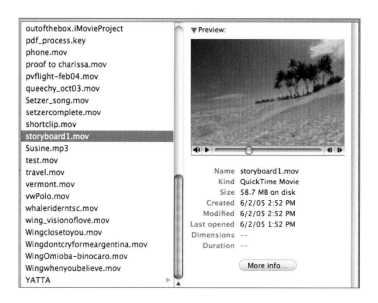

There are a few additional features of iPhoto's Slideshow tool worth mentioning. We won't be using them extensively in this project, but you should feel free to play with them, if you like; doing so might give you some helpful ideas for use later in this project.

The Music button lets you specify music to play along with your slideshow—specifically, music stored in your iTunes music library. We'll be creating some music of our own later, and the music settings applied here won't affect our final movie, but it may be helpful to get a feel for the effect music can have on your show. Click the Music button, check Play Music During Slideshow in the panel that appears, and choose the classical-guitar sample from the menu or pick any song you've loaded in iTunes. Play the slideshow again to see how the accompaniment affects the movie's mood.

There is another way to export your slideshow as a QuickTime movie. Rather than selecting the completed slideshow in the list in the left pane, you can choose the storyboard album in the Source list. Select all the images (Command+A) and then choose Share > Export. This time, you'll be given slightly different choices. First of all, you'll be able to enter customized sizing for your movie. But don't worry—no matter what your customized size is, this setting won't distort the images. It merely scales the QuickTime movie window that frames your slideshow.

Next, you'll notice the option to select an image for the background of the QuickTime window. If you go this route, be sure that the image fits snugly to the same dimensions as your customized window size. Your slideshow will begin with the image you have selected, and all subsequent images will appear on top of it. The last image you see will be the background image. This is a nice way to open and close your little movie, beginning and ending from the same spot, as it were, using it to illustrate how things change…or not.

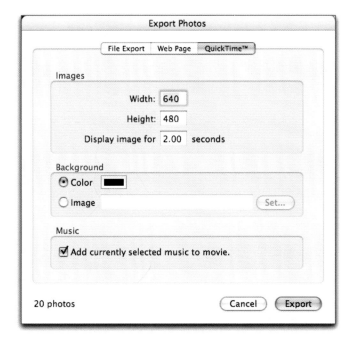

Or you could use a background image that contains your company logo, reinforcing your company brand. The idea here is that if you do choose to use the background image, do so in a way that means something and that adds something to your movie.

There is a drawback to exporting in this fashion, however. Although we have more options, as far as sizing goes, when you watch your slideshow… well, bub, this may just be Apple's way of saying that if you want to be a filmmaker, get ready for disappointment. The transitions are reduced to the default dissolve, and no special effects need apply. Apple seems to be playing a carrot/stick game with us here. Apple gives a little *here* but takes away something from *there*.

But as out-of-the-box designers, we're already used to compromise of our final vision. We can handle it. Even though iPhoto slideshows lose some of the subtlety that we may have invested in their transitions when we export to QuickTime, the skills we've used to create them can be used in iMovie to build QuickTime slideshows that better reflect our higher artistic nature.

Also, we'll have the ability to add sound effects, full-motion video, and a whole arsenal of other features to our simple stories. So *of course* we can handle the compromises that come with creation.

With iPhoto, you can also export a slideshow for use in iDVD. We'll be discussing that later in the chapter. For now, let's make some music.

Putting Down Some Tracks

●●●●●●●

In Hollywood, there is an elite cadre of employed people known as Foley artists. (Actually, employed people in Hollywood are an elite group just by that fact alone.) Named for Jack Foley, a sound editor at Universal Pictures who died in 1967, Foley artists create and match live sounds to the actions of a film. The sound you hear in the audience when fist hits jaw onscreen is more than likely a bunch of celery wrapped in a towel hitting a wooden table. But you don't perceive it as such. Sound and image entwine in your mind, and you perceive a fist hitting a jaw. A punch to the jaw doesn't even make a sound remotely like the sound of celery on wood, but Foley artists long ago figured out, through years of trial and error, that celery-in-towel-hitting-wood makes a sound that we *expect* to hear from a knuckle sandwich.

The sound of a romantic passionate kiss may actually be that of a Foley artist sucking his forearm. But without that subtly added sound texture, a scene could fall flat.

Foley is an extreme case of how noise and sound act as elements of an overall composition on film. Although it's tough to do, try watching a movie or television show, and imagine the scenes without the enhancements of sound effects. Imagine a science-fiction movie that mirrors reality. There is no sound in the vacuum of space, yet when you see the spaceship whiz by, you inevitably hear the whoosh of air. Why? Because without sound to back it up, the film is missing a vital piece of its own design.

Try imagining movies without music. Music is used in so many subtle and not-so-subtle ways in every scene we watch that we don't pay it much attention—at least, not on a conscious level. But mixing a scene with music is as important as having an image there in the first place. In fact, sometimes having just music and no image is more effective than having action and music together.

But how do we lowly mortals—who are not Foley artists, who are not musicians, and who can't even read music—compose and apply music to our movies? I believe the professional technical response to these questions and subclause questions is "Duh-uh. We use GarageBand."

GarageBand is a powerful and intuitive application that works even for those of us without musical ambitions, let alone talent. GarageBand can help you compose, record, arrange, mix, and deliver music from scratch, which is right up our alley. Even though it doesn't bear an iName, it's bundled in the iLife suite that also includes iTunes, iPhoto, and iMovie.

Why is that important to know? The iLife applications have an interoperability and sharing function that makes it easy to exchange the various products of each application, building on one another as though you have a collaborative group of designers hidden inside your Macintosh, running on little gerbil exercise wheels as fast as you want them to.

Sound design has a lot in common with layout and image design. With each discipline, we still have to consider all those things we have been using up to this point: message, audience, use, and delivery. And that one other Rule of Thumb is making negatives into positives, deficits into assets. We sometimes like to call that the "I meant to put that space there" or *lemonade* rule.

Les Paul, the man who lends his name to one of the world's most famous electric guitars, is more than just a musician. He's also a groundbreaking innovator of musical technology. In addition to helping develop the solid-body electric guitar and the pickups that make it work, he invented multitrack recording. This innovation—which allows separate recorded performances to be mixed into a single song or composition—is a supreme example of the lemonade rule. Paul didn't want to have to hire other musicians to record his songs, so he invented multitracking as a means of accompanying himself: He'd record one guitar part and then, while listening to that track, play and record an accompaniment. When he got the second part down, he'd merge it with the first and repeat. Using this approach, Paul created a string of hit records in the 1950s, featuring his multipart "solo" guitar work and vocals by his wife, Mary Ford (who also acted as her own backup singers). Today, multitrack recording is the standard, and dozens (or even hundreds) of separate vocal and instrumental tracks are routinely mixed (and remixed) to create CDs and movie scores.

Les Paul's innovations aren't just examples of making more out of less; they are also intrinsically tied to the software we're about to use. Paul made the first in a series of technological leaps that allow us to compose music right out of the box with our Macs. Techniques that began when he hitched together a couple of dishwasher-size reel-to-reel tape decks are now available, in vastly improved form, in a window on our Macs.

In the case of *our* soundtrack, the big deficit may be musicianship. So we must figure out a way to get around lack of talent and knowledge, and still make beautiful music. And when we have a handle on how to do that, we'll know how to get to Carnegie Hall.

Those of you who are musicians, even you piddlers and pickers on the guitar out there, are excepted from the comment above. You won't learn anything from us here that will improve your chops, but the basic instructions we show you here may give you insight into some new techniques for applying your talents. At the very least—and this is nothing to sneeze at, mind you—you'll get a quick start on GarageBand.

Now, about those directions to the concert hall—you *do* know how to get to Carnegie Hall, don't you?

Practice. Practice. Practice.

Exploring GarageBand

To begin, let's get acquainted with GarageBand and its interface. It's slightly more complex than most of the other applications we have been using thus far. Find GarageBand in your Applications folder, and open it.

GarageBand also takes more processor power than most of your out-of-the-box applications, so be patient as it starts up.

The workspace is divided into three main sections. We have the Tracks and Track Mixing controls on the left. To the right is the timeline. And below both of those are a series of buttons that, when clicked, open various drop-down drawers for the Loop Browser, Track Info, and Track Editor. This may be the only time you may rue your decision to buy the 12-inch screen. When things start to get going in GarageBand, you'll find yourself scrolling more than you're used to in other applications.

Because GarageBand is potentially one of those black holes that will suck you in along with all your free time, your concentration, and your enthusiasm (with good results, mind you), we'll spend some time going through its features and tools.

The timeline takes up the most real estate in the GarageBand window and is similar to the timeline you'll soon see in iMovie. Each *track,* or section of music, is represented as a horizontal band in the timeline, with its start position on the left and its end on the right. The small triangle at the top of the timeline is called the playhead; it moves from left to right as a song plays. Drag the playhead to any spot in the timeline to work on a particular segment of music.

You can change the viewing scale of the timeline with the slider in the bottom-left section of the track pane. Sliding it all the way to the left always fits your entire song in the timeline, no matter how long it is. Moving the slider right "zooms in" for more detailed work.

By default, the ruler in GarageBand's timeline measures time in musical *beats,* dividing the duration by its *tempo* in beats per minute *(bpm).* You can change the tempo by clicking Tempo in the groovy faux-LCD time readout in the window below the timeline. You can also change the GarageBand timeline to measure elapsed time in seconds by clicking the grayed-out clock-face icon that's surreptitiously located to the left of the musical note in the LCD readout. Because iMovie uses standard time units, it be helpful to switch to this mode, but for now, we'll stick with beats.

No matter where your playhead is, you can return to Beat 1 by pressing the Home key on your computer keyboard. If you're on a laptop, just press Return.

But we don't need to go too deeply into GarageBand here. We're project-oriented, and we need to get something done. So the niceties of the application will have to wait for your free time. We have work to do. We have to make a soundtrack for our film.

Now, ordinarily, we would put our scenes together and then make our soundtrack accordingly. We'd have our scenes done, and we'd compose to them. The timing would be specific to the action in the movie. But we're going to do it slightly differently here. We have our storyboard, and we'll take a side trip to iMovie soon to place images. Then we'll return to GarageBand and compose.

Musical design decisions

As in any creative venture, we have certain considerations to take into account so we can make the appropriate design decision. Audio is no exception. We made reference to this at the beginning of this section, when we tried to imagine movies without music. Let's try an experiment. Turn on a television set, and find a movie. Turn down the sound. Now start up iTunes, and choose a song. After a bit of time, change the song. All this time, pay close attention to how the music affects the goings-on of the scene on the screen.

If you happen to be lucky enough to have an iPod handy, you can try this just walking down a crowded street. The music sets the tone. So when we're creating the soundtrack, we have the power to do the same according to our intentions, or point of view.

As a way of further illustrating this aspect of design—*sound design*, if you will—we'll make two distinct tunes in GarageBand and later apply them to our movie.

Before we get too far along in GarageBand, remind yourself of the run time for the preliminary QuickTime movie we exported from iPhoto. This will give us a good idea of how long we have to labor in the dark hole we're about to enter. (And I mean that in a good way.)

When GarageBand starts up, you'll have one track showing in the time-line, but it will be empty. In the Track pane to the left, you'll see the default setup with Grand Piano. There is nothing in the timeline, however, until we play something.

We'll start with manual input. Choose Window > Keyboard (Command+K). Now a small keyboard appears. Even if you've never touched a finger to a real piano, click the key that says C3. That note is the same note as mid-dle C on a real piano keyboard. You can tell by looking at the blue outline just above the live keys you've just clicked. The blue area defines the area on a full keyboard that you can see within the small keyboard window.

Now click-drag across the whole keyboard. Wow. Just like a real piano. But you'll note that no notes showed up in your timeline. Look down at the bottom of the GarageBand window. Notice the circular button with the dimmed red light inside it. That is the Record button. But don't touch it yet. We have a few more things to look at first.

Double-click the track name Grand Piano. The Track Info window opens. Our Grand Piano doesn't have to remain; we can use virtually any instru-ment we like. In the left pane of the Track Info window, click Guitars, and then, in the right pane, select Classical Acoustic. Now go back to the key-board and click. Drag across several keys. You'll hear not just the notes, but the internote slide on the fretboard as well. If you're tempted to experiment with that right now, go ahead. But first, make a note of the time. Check your watch. Try not to spend too much time futzing around. We still have music to make.

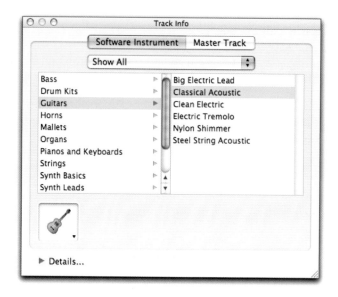

If you're using GarageBand 2, you have another musical-input option. Choose Window > Musical Typing (Command+Shift+K), and instead of the virtual piano keyboard, you'll see a picture of the Mac keyboard with piano keys matched to the letter keys.

Unlike the Keyboard screen, which is limited to one clickable note at a time, Musical Typing lets you play as many as eight notes at the same time so you can use it to play chords.

If you feel strongly about making music, of course, you can (for a few bucks less than $100) buy a popular USB musical keyboard (find it at www.apple.com) and avoid the whole limitation problem. Then all you need do is practice.

Musical Typing also adds a Pitch Bend control you can use to make notes rise or drop in pitch after you play them. We can wait ten minutes while you experiment with this.

Waiting.

Still waiting.

Humming. Looking at watch.

Whistling now. Tapping foot.

Looking at watch again.

OK. Done so soon? Great. Ready to move on.

If you're actually a musician, you can use the plus-sign button in the bottom-left corner to add another track for other (virtual) Software Instruments, or if you have an electric guitar or other instrument you can plug into an amplifier, you can plug it into your Mac's sound-input (Microphone) jack instead and record a Real Instrument track.

Because we're assuming that we don't have any hope of playing music ourselves manually, we'll go to our next alternative: prefabricated loops.

GarageBand gives us zillions of them to choose among. First, we'll have to find them.

Click the Eye button at the bottom of the main window, henceforth known as the Loop Browser button. The Loop Browser opens as a drawer to the main window. The vast array of instrument types can be viewed either as buttons (the default view) or, if you click the View button in the bottom-left corner, in a columnar listing. Leaving the view as buttons, click the All Drums button.

Search the listing that appears in the right pane for Classic Rock Beat 02. Clicking that name will play the loop so you can preview it. Classic Rock Beat 02 might be a classic, but it sure sounds slow. We can fix that. Notice the digital meter just above the Loop Browser drawer. On the right is a number that says Tempo. While the beat is playing, click Tempo; a slider will appear. Slide the number up until it reaches 180. Now it should sound more like a basic rock beat.

You should get the idea that you can adjust any of these loops to suit the tempo you're looking for.

Click Classic Rock Beat 02 to make it stop. Sigh relief and then click-drag the name from the Loop Browser to the main window. Note that if you drag your mouse over the timeline, the playhead will follow your mouse, and when you release your mouse button, the loop will drop in at that point in the timeline. So to be sure to start the beat at the very beginning, drag your mouse all the way to the left, and release.

Before we start stringing loops together, here's an overview of how they work. You don't need to know all this to use GarageBand, but understanding it can help you make decisions about how and when to use different kinds of loops.

Software Instrument loops and tracks (with green musical-note icons in the GarageBand Loop Library and timeline) are based on a technology called MIDI (Musical Instrument Digital Interface), which lets electronic musical devices share data and control one another. MIDI is used (in a very, very limited way) by Keyboard Typing and GarageBand's onscreen Keyboard window; adding MIDI-controller hardware to your Mac gives you far greater control over Software Instruments. (Controllers range from sub-$100 USB musical keyboards to pro rigs that can cost more than your car—no matter what you drive.) Translating Software Instrument tracks into sound takes a lot of processing horsepower.

Loops with blue waveform icons are Real Instrument tracks. In Garage-Band-speak, a Real Instrument is anything that generates a signal you can feed to an amplifier, including electric guitars and basses, pickup-equipped horns (and accordions, didgeridoos, and so on), turntables, and microphones. You can't edit individual notes in a Real Instrument track, the way you can with a Software Instrument, but you can use Garage-Band to cut them apart, splice them together, and process them with digital effects such as reverb and distortion. Real Instrument loops and tracks are digital audio files; they take up a lot of disk space (and RAM, during recording any playback). Thanks to the Mac's dedicated digital audio hardware, manipulating them doesn't make huge demands on your Mac CPU.

Your basic drum track has a green musical-note icon, so it's a Software Instrument loop, as will be most of the loops we'll be working with from here out.

But first, let's do something to extend our drumbeat longer than the few seconds the loop runs now. In the timeline, position your mouse in the top-right part of the green drum track. Your pointer becomes a circular arrow and line. While the pointer is in that state, click-drag to the right. The track extends, repeating itself up to the point where you release. Drag the loop out to measure 13 on the timeline. Notice the small indents in the loop. Each indent is a complete measure. If you were to leave it off before a complete measure, the loop wouldn't be complete.

After you've dragged to measure 13, press your spacebar. The beat plays on. The problem is, it doesn't stop just because the loop does; it goes on and on. So to have it repeat itself from the beginning to that point and back again to the beginning, click the Cycle button in the playback controls at the bottom.

When you click the Cycle button, the Beat measure in the timeline adds a lower level of measurements. Click-drag your mouse across from 0 to 5, and a yellow area appears. That zone is the cycle region that will loop continuously when you click Play. Try it.

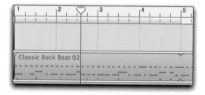

This allows you to work out one pattern of music without resorting to stop-and-start clicks and unnecessary mouse movements. In this instance, we made the cycle region 5, but you can make it as long or short an interval as you please.

Now let's add a bass track to the song. Click the Loop Browser button. Scroll through the myriad bass offerings to Walking Upright Bass 01. Press your spacebar and then click Walking Upright Bass 01. The drumbeat will play, and your choice of bass will play along with it. Try a few other bass lines. Check out Rock Bass 09, for instance. See how with the same drumbeat, but different bass line, the song builds in a completely different direction. The temptations of the black hole are starting to beckon. But ignore them for now.

Go back to Walking Upright Bass 01, and drag it into the timeline as its own track. But this time, instead of dragging the bass line to Beat 1, put it at Beat 3. This way, we open with a drumbeat and add to it with the bass line, accumulating sound rather than throwing it all at the listener at once—a *design decision*.

Now drag the bass line to Beat 13, so that it ends at the same point as the drum. You may want to save your song now.

We have a rhythm. Well, we have the beginnings of a rhythm. Now we need a melody. Open the Loop Browser, and click the Piano button. Select Classic Rock Piano 03. Drag the selection to its own track, beginning at Beat 5. Now extend Classic Rock Piano 03 another measure so that it ends on Beat 13. Test the song so far.

Go back to the Loop Browser, and select Delicate Piano 01. Place Delicate Piano 01 in the top Grand Piano track, at Beat 9. When you preview the song, you many not hear the delicate piano, but we can do something about that. In the Track Mixer, maximize the volume on the grand piano. Now bring the volumes of the drum kit, the bass, and the other piano down to halfway.

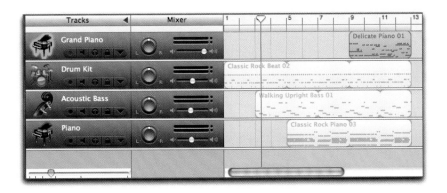

Believe it or not, you're mixing a song. Now select all the tracks at once. Option-drag them so that they end not at Beat 13 but at Beat 21. Make any adjustments to the parts so that they end at the same point. Garage-Band won't allow any overlaps within individual tracks, so don't worry about that.

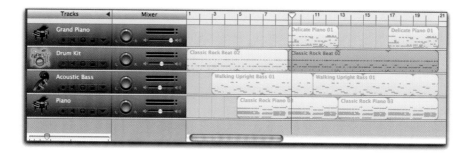

This is a nice, lyrical, ballady song so far. But it still lacks an edge. Let's add one more piece to the puzzle before we connect the pieces and export. This time, we'll use a different method to find the right instrument. Open the Loop Browser, and in the bottom-left section of the window, choose the column-display option rather than the button method of viewing.

Select By Moods, and then, in the column, select Intense.

Unlike images, which can be categorized technically in such terms as RGB or CMYK, or fonts, which can be categorized in technical terms such as serif or ornamental, music loops in GarageBand have the added feature of "mood" categories. GarageBand can't account for every mood in the human-musical gamut (or whatever you want to call it), of course, but that brings up a good point.

Just as in iPhoto, where we can apply keywords to images and even invent our own, we can define and add our own designations for loop moods in GarageBand. But this is a digression. At this point, we can use the existing classifications, but keep this option in mind for future projects.

In the next column (note that it's now named the Intense column), choose Guitars. Also note that there is a number in parentheses after each item, showing how many loops fit the genre description we're searching for. Guitars has 8. Choose Edgy Rock Guitar 14, and drag it into the timeline. Now preview the song again.

Nice intro, delicate and soothing. But then, the Edgy Rock Guitar breaks the mood. Oops. We're big enough to admit when we've made a mistake. The Edgy Rock Guitar might work somewhere else, but not in this song. Let's get rid of it. Select the track, and choose Track > Delete Track (Command+Delete).

The song still needs something. Maybe rock-guitar edginess wasn't it. But because we're already here, let's try out a few of the other so-called intense loops. Try Acoustic Picking 07. Drag it in to the timeline at Beat 13, and extend it to Beat 21.

Hey, it works. It gives us an added texture that grounds the song and takes off the Pollyanna polish. It's a keeper.

Save your file.

Up till now, we've been building the song with no real awareness of length. We've been concentrating on getting a particular sound. But practicalities must take precedence. We plan on having a film of about a minute in length. So we have to find out a few facts. How long is our song so far? And is this the only soundtrack we'll be using?

We can see exactly how long our song is so far by clicking the digital readout bar. By default, it reads out in beats and measures. But if we click the small grayed clock icon, it becomes an exact time measurement. For our purposes, that will work fine.

Drag the playhead to Beat 21 on the timeline, and you'll see that our song is approximately 35 seconds long.

Let's refer to our storyboard slideshows for an idea of how long this song should be.

If we use something akin to what I'm showing above, we'll start with water images, move on to the ship in the storm, and then go on to jagged rocks on a shoreline. So far, none of that seems to fit our ballad. So maybe we won't open with the music. Maybe, when we get to it in iMovie, we'll use something else.

So we've made at least one design decision that moves us forward. Our song doesn't need to be as long as the whole film and, in fact, should come in around midway, when the storm subsides and the island life is good. We can explore this further in iMovie.

Right now, let's finish off this song. Let's make the song around 45 seconds total. To do that, we'll have to know where 45 seconds is on the timeline. Drag just the playhead across the timeline, and watch the readout. It looks to be around 26.5 on the old beat measure, so that's what we'll head for.

Select all the tracks that end at Beat 21. Place your mouse in the top-right portion of any of them. The pointer becomes the loop icon. Drag across to Beat 26.5.

Now let's give it a little more of a story. See, we're dealing with the same structures in each aspect of our moviemaking. The song shouldn't just roll on and on; it should have a story too. That means a beginning, a middle, and an end. We have established the beginning and the middle. Now let's define the end.

Make sure you've deselected all your tracks. Place your mouse in the top-right section of the drumbeat track, and retract the length of the track from Beat 26.5 to Beat 25.

Retract Classic Rock Piano 03 to Beat 24. Do the same with Acoustic Picking. Bring the bass track back to 26. Now extend the Grand Piano track to Beat 30. Here's what it should look like.

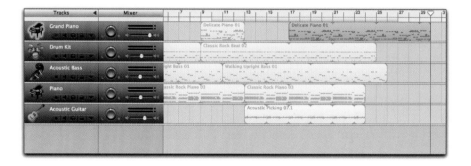

Take a listen. The individual dropoffs of the instruments reflect the opening of the song, which has just the beat, then the bass, and then the other instruments. This *denouement* of the song gives it balance, much the same way we balance a layout on a flier. It's weighted on either side, but the sides are not necessarily mirror images.

We have one last thing to do before we finish our song: We want a master track to control the overall volume of the combination of tracks. It will give us broad control of the presentation.

Choose Track > Show Master Track (Command+B). The master track appears at the bottom of the window. With the master track, we can adjust the overall volume as well as the pitch of the song. While working with master volume, scroll across to Beat 29, and click the volume line at Beat 28.5. A purple sphere appears on the line. Now click the line again, this time at Beat 30. Drag the point at Beat 30 downward. By doing this, you're creating a quick fadeout.

You have probably noticed that each track also has its own volume and mute controls. So you can and should adjust each instrument individually while constructing your overall sound. This takes a lot of practice, however, so take some time to experiment. (Headphones help, too.)

Now listen to the whole song. We could go on and on adding to the song, adding elements and creating sound layers. But we just want to get an idea here of how easy it is to create a professional-sounding background soundtrack or song.

Save your song file. Then choose File > Export to iTunes. The song will appear in your iTunes Library. In iTunes, select the song, and press Command I. In the Summary, you'll note that the song is an AIFF file, which means it takes up a lot of space. Close the Info window. In iTunes, make sure the song is still selected, and choose Advanced > Convert Selection to MP3. Now you'll have two identical song names in your Library list. The AIFF file, however, is about 9.3 MB, whereas the MP3 file is only 1.3 MB.

Select one of the files, and choose File > Show Song File (Command+R). A Finder window will open, and both songs will be there. You can choose to throw the AIFF file in the Trash. We won't be needing it as long as we have the MP3 version. For our purposes, we don't need the bulk of the AIFF file, and the sound quality of the MP3 is fine.

A change of tune

Let's make an alternative song that has a completely different mood and tempo from the one we've just created.

In GarageBand, open a new file. GarageBand will ask us to create a new project. Name the file Edgier. This version should go much quicker now that we're familiar with the basic GarageBand controls.

Open the Loop Browser, use the column view, and choose By Instruments >All Drums > Dark > Electronic Drum Beat 03. Drag the loop to its own track. The track will extend to Beat 9.

Now go back to the Loop Browser, and choose By Instruments > All Drums > Distorted > Effected Drum Kit 05. Drag that loop to its own track. This track extends only to Beat 3 on the timeline, so drag it (place your mouse in the top-right corner) to Beat 9.

Click the Cycle button, and drag the cycle region from 1 to 9. Now press the spacebar to play the beat.

Go back to the Loop Browser, and choose By Instruments > Elec Guitar > Dark > Secret Agent 04. Drag the loop to its own track. Place the loop so that it starts at Beat 3, and extend it to Beat 11.

Next, choose By Instruments > Elec Guitar > Distorted > Edgy Rock Guitar 14, and place the loop to start at Beat 7. Then extend the electronic
beats (both of them) to Beat 11. Turn off the Cycle region, and listen to the
whole song so far.

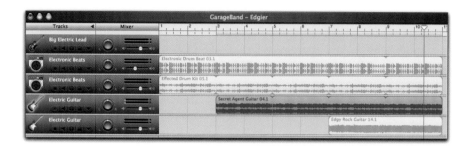

OK. Let's add just a little more to this edgy soundtrack and then finish. In
the Loop Browser, choose By Instruments > Bass > Elec Bass > Alternative Rock Bass 04. Drag the loop to its own track, starting at Beat 1 and
extending all the way to Beat 11.

This ought to give us a stark-contrast alternative to play with in iMovie.
This song is only 20 seconds long, but we'll be able to loop it in iMovie.

Let's finish this off by exporting to iTunes and converting the song to MP3
as we did with the earlier ballad.

We now have two very different soundtrack choices for our short movie.
Here, it is important to remember our Rules of Thumb and consider what
our original intentions are for the movie. Who is our intended audience?
How do we want them to feel? Are they strangers to whom we want to
sell something? Or are they our grandparents, with whom we want to
share our recent ordeal? How will these two disparate audiences react to
our different types of music? These are design decisions that nag at our
consciences and after a while become almost intuitive. It's at that point
that we start to define our point of view. It's at this point that we climb
out of our black hole and realize that we've completed two of the first
three necessary ingredients for making a movie.

Please remember that just as in any of the other applications we've used
in this book, there are many more possibilities and features of GarageBand

that we haven't touched on. But we're looking at how these applications work as spokes in the wheel of a project, not as projects in and of themselves.

It's time to quit GarageBand and make room for our next step.

Putting It All Together

●●●●●●●

Without the benefit of a video camera, we're about to make a short movie using still images that we've culled from various and sundry resources. We're deep in the iLife suite of applications at this point. So far, we've used iPhoto to sort through our images and come up with some sample slideshows that work as a storyboarding application.

We went on to GarageBand, where we made two short and diverse musical files. Then we exported them in the AIFF file format (the kind you find on commercial CDs) to iTunes, where we converted them for size to MP3. And now we're about to step into iMovie, where we will put the elements together in a coherent manner.

As we said earlier, the beauty of these applications is their integration and interoperability. This next step is proof of it.

Open iMovie. Create a new project, and name it Out of the Box.

iMovie's interface is among the simplest you'll find. iMovie is one of those applications that any 11-year-old nearby can explain to you if you don't understand it. Sometimes, we get so caught up in our complex ideas and convoluted lives that we forget what it's like to work in simplicity. iMovie is a simple program that does very complex things. Just as in other forms of design, we should try to remind ourselves to simplify before we get carried away with other concerns.

The iMovie interface is laid out in front of you. The big black space taking up most of the screen is the iMovie Monitor. This is where you'll run clips or preview your movie as you go. The Clip pane on the right contains small empty holders that show thumbnails of movie clips when they are imported.

Just below the pane are the pane buttons. Clicking these buttons will change the contents of the pane. By default, you're showing the Clips pane. When you click (as you will momentarily) the Photos pane button, the pane above will show you the photo images you have available to use in the movie.

Click the Photos button now. The pane is divided into an top and bottom part. You may recognize the top part from iPhoto. The Ken Burns Effect here has slightly more complex controls than those in iPhoto, but it's essentially the same thing.

The bottom part of the pane is a pop-up menu that defaults to your iPhoto Library. Click the pop-up window to reveal all the albums in iPhoto.

We'll go over the other panes as we need them. But first, let's look at the other controls we'll be working with.

Along the bottom of the iMovie window is the timeline. The timeline here has two basic viewing modes. You can choose to build your project from clip to clip, in Clip mode, or go the more traditional route and use Timeline mode. You'll find the toggle buttons for either method just below the Monitor window.

To the right of those buttons is the Mode switch, which toggles iMovie between Camera mode and Edit mode. Because we're not importing or transferring any movies to an input device at this time, we'll stick to Edit mode. If we did have a video or still camera attached to our computer, we would use Camera mode to import the raw content into iMovie. In the case of video, any clips (any periods of footage between recording pauses) would be imported and added to the Clip pane.

> NOTE: THE LAST SENTENCE IS TRUE OF MAGIC IMOVIE MODE IN IMOVIE 5, BUT IN EARLIER VERSIONS OF THE PROGRAM (AND IN MANY PRACTICAL APPLICATIONS OF IMOVIE 5), CLIPS ARE DEFINED AND IMPORTED MANUALLY, BY SCRUBBING THROUGH CAMERA CONTENTS IN THE CAMERA WINDOW AND USING THE RECORD BUTTON TO START AND STOP THE IMPORT PROCESS.

Centered just below the Monitor window are the playback controls. To the right of these controls is the master volume. Don't believe me? Ask your 11-year-old.

We've done much of the heavy lifting already by preparing our photos in iPhoto. So to get started, all we have to do it import our images.

Back in the Photos pane, select storyboard in the albums listing. Now prepare yourself for ease of use. If we've done our work properly, the order we set for the images back in iPhoto is the same order in which we'll see the images now in the preview window just below the pop-up menu. Select all the images by clicking the first image and then scrolling down to the last image and Shift-clicking. All the images should have the light-blue selection keyline around them.

Now carefully drag the group into the timeline. The images will automatically import into iMovie, *in the order in which we arranged them in the album.*

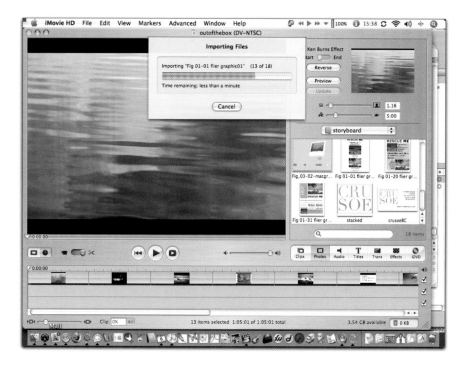

When the import is complete, reset the playhead to the beginning, and click Play. Make sure everything is in the order you originally planned. See whether the image order makes sense. There won't be any transitions as yet; neither will there be any soundtrack. By default, the Ken Burns Effect will zoom into your images before moving in a fast cut to the next. But we'll adjust all these things in a moment.

Select the first image in the timeline. Click the Photos button. The Ken Burns Effect is checked. Uncheck it, and click the Update button.

If you replay the movie now, the initial image simply sits there for around 4-1/2 seconds. In the Photos pane, you can adjust how long the image appears. Next to the Slower icon (which is represented as a tortoise) is a time-input area. Make the time 5:00, for 5 seconds. Click the Ken Burns Effect to turn it on, promptly unclick it, and then click Update. Now the still will last 5 seconds.

But we really do want movement on this image, especially if it is an image of water. We don't want just the basic generic zoom. Water doesn't move like that; it moves laterally. So we'll use the Ken Burns Effect to good use, simulating the movement of water. We want to tell a story here, and our story begins at sea.

Make sure you have the first image selected in the timeline. In the Photo pane, click the Ken Burns Effect once more. Toggle the Start/End switch to Start. In the image preview to the right, you can see how your effects will work. Drag the scale to 3.00. Now place your mouse in the middle of the image preview, and pull the image to the right until you can see the edge on the left. Be sure to keep the image in frame.

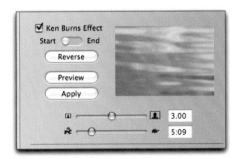

Next, we have to define the endpoint of the effect. As we said earlier, we're trying to simulate how water flows. We don't want to zoom in on it; we want it to move across the screen. If you recall, we did this earlier in iPhoto. The process is simple, but more important, it's a design decision as well. This kind of movement has a technical term that we've all heard: *panning*. We are going to pan across the image, or move from left to right or right to left. So click the Start/End switch to End, and we'll define the endpoint.

The scale will undoubtedly change. Slide it to the same number you set for the Start, which in this case was 3.00. Now do the opposite of what you did for the Start point—that is, place your mouse in the preview frame and drag the image to the left instead of the right. Drag until you see the edge of the image, and leave it so that the image completely covers the frame, without any edge showing. Now click Update. Click the Preview button to check your work.

We can do one of two things now. Either we can select all the remaining images in the timeline (Shift-click across the timeline) and, with all of them selected, go to the Photos pane and unclick the Ken Burns Effect; or we can take them on individually.

This isn't a big design decision, but one of production. Either way, we're going to go through the timeline image by image and make specific adjustments to each one. It's simply a matter of whether we want the Ken Burns Effect to be our default position or to have the images be static.

If you're having trouble deciding, follow me. Select all (except for the first image), and select and deselect the Ken Burns Effect. Now click Update.

Here is the timeline as I've conceived it from the images in the storyboard. There are five images of sea and weather, followed by an image of a ship being tossed by a storm and then an image of a rocky shore (this was taken from the Black and White Desktop pictures in the library of Mac OS X 10.4).

Here is the list of images, once again, that we used for the storyboard:

> From Desktop Pictures (including Black and White, found in Macintosh HD/Library/Desktop Pictures): Tranquil Surface, Lightning, Pier, Sea Mist, Stones, Zen Garden.

> From screen grabs and other projects: Beach images 1 and 2 (from the flier exercises), screen grabs of three flier versions, one screen grab of your logo, one screen grab of your business card, one picture of fruit or vegetables

> From the Web, we need two images: a ship in a storm and an image of the Macintosh

You don't have to have the exact same images, but something close to them so that we can have an understanding of how we're going to tell our story. Refer to the figure earlier in this chapter with thumbnails from the storyboard album.

If you would like to have a better sense of the images in the timeline, toggle Timeline view to Clips view.

In the timeline, select the second image. In our story, the second image is Lightning. It's here that we can start making inroads into our point of view, even before we integrate our soundtrack. Our choices of effects and transitions will help set the tone for the whole story. So let's experiment a little and see what we can come up with.

Lightning is now 5 seconds in duration and has no Ken Burns Effect. A storm, unlike flowing water, can come up on you or move away from you. So we can try zooming the image rather than panning it. The timeline can be in either Clip or Timeline mode for this; it doesn't matter.

Select Lightning, and go to the Photos pane. Turn on the Ken Burns Effect. Scale your Start point to 1.40 or thereabouts. Now switch to the End point, and scale that to 2.5. While setting up the End point, adjust the image in the preview so that it centers on the lightning bolt. We want to convey the drama of the storm coming directly toward us. We've begun to establish a point of view. But in filmmaking, there's a point of view and then there's *point of view*. Click Update when you've finished adjusting the Ken Burns Effect.

If we preview the movie now, we'll see that there is a hard cut between the first and second images. This might not be what we want. Let's consider how we want to fashion our story. Certainly, storms do come up quickly at sea. But sometimes they also give us warning. They mix the waters up a little, and the wind picks up. So to reflect the change from rolling seas to roiling seas, we should apply a suitable transition.

We find a very complete set of transitions by clicking the Transition-pane button (it appears as Trans in the iMovie Window). Scroll down to Cross Dissolve. Cross Dissolve is one of the simplest and most effective ways of transitioning two related images. Select the first and second images (Tranquil Water and Lightning), and click Preview in the Transition pane. Adjust the speed of the transition with the slider just below the thumbnail preview. Somewhere around 2:00 (2 seconds) allows our eyes to take in the tranquility moving to the storm, which is what we want our story to say.

Here's how we'll apply this transition. Select Cross Dissolve in the Transition list, and drag it down to the timeline, placing it between the two images you want it to affect.

Preview your movie in the Monitor. Does it transition nicely? Good. Let the preview go on to the next image. Does that work as well? If not, you can change and rearrange some of the images. We have Pier in the third position, for example. Although Pier is a beautiful image, it doesn't have much to do with our ship at sea. We want to show the ship in the storm. Then we can use Pier…or perhaps not. We'll see in a moment.

Now you'll see why we have the alternative modes of viewing the timeline. If you're in Time mode, it's a little more difficult to rearrange your clips. They slide back and forth according to time, not order. It can be done, but why wrestle with the program? Switch over to Clip mode in the timeline first.

In this mode, we can click, drag, and drop our clips in the order that works best. You can also see that even though we had our storyboard, when we finally put some transitions and effects on our images in context, we could change our minds. Nothing is fixed until we deliver the final piece.

So let's rearrange the clips. Put the Pier image two images after the ship-at-sea image, in the fifth position.

Preview your movie so far, stopping after the fourth image. Tranquil sea, storm approaching, ship tossed, impending rocks—that's starting to give us a story. The ship and the rocks have no transitions applied to them; they're hard cuts. And that makes sense as a design decision. We want to show the sharp contrast and imminent danger that the storm has put us in. Mind you, this is a silent movie up to now, so we want the relationships of the images, and the transitions from one image to the next, to carry as much dramatic weight as possible. When we apply sound and sound effects, we'll enhance the drama.

Do this for both the ship and the rocks. Now let's shorten the time for each clip, again, to emphasize the danger. Here's what we'll do. First, let's apply Ken Burns Effect to the ship image. Make it a slight zoom, and give the whole effect 2 seconds. Update your image with the effect.

The image of the rocks (Sea Mist) is next. Let's apply the Ken Burns Effect again, but this time, let's do a closeup pan of the shot, also for 2 seconds. Apply that effect and then preview your film.

(You should be saving your file intermittently. But you don't need to be reminded of that.)

To increase the drama a little, let's repeat the ship and rock images. In Clip view, select the image you want to copy (in this case, the ship at sea), and Option-drag the image into the new position. It will look as though you're lifting it out of its former position, but when you release the mouse button, you'll see that it's actually duplicated itself.

Now we've repeated the impending doom of the ship and the rocks....

Right after the last rocks image is the pier in the mist. Apply a reverse zoom to it. That means, start the Ken Burns Effect from a closeup and end with a full shot.

The hard cuts work well for the danger, but now we want to introduce the island. The island represents a safe place. We want to convey that we wash up to safety. So again, we'll use a softer transition.

From Pier to our placard Island definition, apply a cross-dissolve. Go to the Transition pane, select Cross Dissolve, and drag it to the space between the two images.

Apply a reverse Ken Burns Effect to the Island placard, and give it around 4-½ to 5 seconds. That will juxtapose the drama of the rocks with the tran-quility of the island. Always remember to apply or update the effects you choose.

See how each decision we make here relates to how we want to tell a story.

The next section of images relates to island life. You could almost say we're about to go into the next *chapter* in the story. Funny you should say that, because movies delivered on DVD, which this will become, also use the chapter metaphor. Chapters on a DVD allow you to make shortcuts, which you sometimes see as scene selections in the menu. We can save ourselves some time and do that now.

Click the iDVD Pane button. At the top of the new pane is the title iDVD Chapter Markers. What a coincidence.

In the timeline, scroll to the first image. Now, in the iDVD pane, click the Add Chapter button.

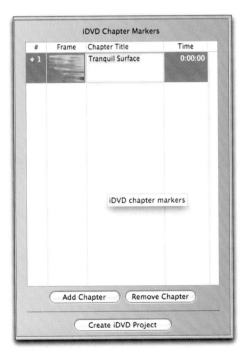

We can rename the first chapter, but we really don't have to. Tranquil Surface is a good name for the opening.

In the timeline, select the Island placard. In the iDVD pane, click Add Chapter. Rename the chapter Island Life.

Now we have two chapter markers, which will come in handy when we set this up for burning a DVD.

The Island Life chapter should last for seven images. It should end where we place the screen grab of the Macintosh. We'll call that chapter Enter the Macintosh, but don't set it yet. You won't know exactly where it should start until you get a little farther along and see how your transitions and images arrange themselves.

The Island Life chapter tells the story of getting along on the deserted beach. We show the island, some beach pebbles, sand, fish, fruit, and beach chairs. It's almost a vacation. And that's the feeling we want to convey.

Choose the appropriate transitions and presentations without my lead, and see what you come up with. Don't be afraid, however, to experiment with different transitions. Try an overlap if you find a cross-dissolve tedious. Apply a wipe, if you must. But remember this: The transitions should serve the images, the images serve the story, and the order of the images serves the point of view. Bear that in mind as you progress through this chapter.

We'll be waiting at the beginning of the next one.

Hmmm.

Waiting.

Still waiting.

Flipping a coin.

Humming. Looking at watch.

Squinting into the sun.

Whistling now.

Tapping foot.

Looking at watch again.

Reading a newspaper online.

Checking email.

Oh…ready so soon?

Great.

Start the new chapter, Enter the Macintosh. Select the screen grab of the Macintosh. In the iDVD pane, click Add Chapter, and name the chapter.

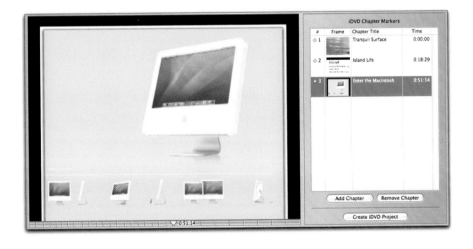

We want to establish a different pace now. The story so far is that we've been shipwrecked, washed up on a deserted island, relaxed, ate, swam, caught fish. Now we're ready to get off the island, and we're going to use the Mac to help us. Do we want anticipation? Do we want urgency? We want to pick up the pace but have a positive aspect to it, not a thriller aspect and impending doom.

So we'll shorten the time each image takes, and we'll choose our transitions to be faster and sharper. Not too sharp, mind you,—not hard cuts.

To emphasize that the Macintosh is the tool we used to create the fliers, let's duplicate the Macintosh image between each of the flier images. Leave the first image of the Mac at 4 or 5 seconds.

All the ensuing duplicates, however, should be fast, taking no more than a second and a half. The first image is a beauty shot; it establishes the Macintosh. All the others are reminders; they're cogs in the wheels of progress. That's what we want to convey. That's the design decision.

So place three duplicate images of the Macintosh on your timeline after each screen grab of each flier.

When the images in place, select them starting with the first Mac image and ending with the last. Open the Transitions pane. Choose Push, adjust the speed of the transition to around half a second, and click Apply.

Preview your movie thus far. Does it tell your story? Almost.

Let's add a new chapter marker after the last Macintosh image. Call it Business Development, because that's what we did. We developed a logo and a business card.

Now go back to the Transitions pane, and select the Wash In transition. Place the transition between the last Macintosh image and the image of your logo.

Place the Overlap transition between your logo and the image of the business card. We want to emphasize the product of our adventure, which is the business—hence, the representation of that as the business card. So we'll let the eye settle on that image for a few more seconds. In the Photos pane, adjust the timing of the business-card image to 6 seconds. As we now know, that's quite a long time for an image. So maybe we want to apply an effect that lets it stay with us and gives it the dramatic import we so desperately want to convey.

Before we do that, duplicate the last image, and put the duplicate at the end of the movie as it now stands. To duplicate the image in this instance, select it, copy, and paste. You'll have two business-card images side by side in the timeline.

Open the heretofore-unopened Effects pane. We haven't opened the Effects pane until now, and for a reason: We've thus far relied on the power of our images and their transitions to help tell our story in the manner we want. Effects sometimes draw so much attention to themselves that they detract from images rather than enhance them. In this case, however, we want to use effects as *part of the story*. Remember, this is as rudimentary a film-making process as we can muster, but that doesn't mean it has to be without integrity. We take all the elements and the design decisions we make very seriously and consider each step in our creative process with an eye toward the project's overall intent.

So we choose to use a particular effect here because it *works* in our story.

Scroll down to Fog. You can play with the Effect In/Effect Out controls to suit your taste. Note that the effect delays the introduction of the effect. So you get a chance to see the image undisturbed for a moment; then the fog rolls in.

Apply the effect. Preview it, and then apply the "Cross Dissolve" transition between the duplicates.

We're almost done working with our images. Two final items need to be inserted. The first is a balancing image. In the spirit of good symmetry, we'll add a duplicate of the tranquil sea image at the very end. Then we'll add titles. You can't have a film if you don't have an end credit, now, can you?

So instead of duplicating the first image in the movie by Option-dragging or copying and pasting, we'll use one more method. Open the Photos pane, locate the image, and drag it onto the timeline. That was easy. Put the Cross Dissolve transition between the foggy business card and the tranquil water.

Situate the playhead at the very end of the movie. Open the Titles pane. You can experiment with various types of titles, but you don't want to contradict the style of the film we've made so far.

With that in mind, select Drifting, choose a font that suits your taste, and type a title for the film.

Preview your film. If it works, we're ready to move on to adding a soundtrack. If there are adjustments, such as transitions and length of time for images, we should make them now.

So far, the movie is quiet. It has a particular feel. It almost has a voice. But it's not obvious. So click the Audio-pane button.

The Audio pane links directly to your iTunes music library. You could apply any song you have in that library to your movie. But after all the time you took to create your own musical soundtrack earlier in this chapter, why not give your own creativity a shot and see how it stands up?

Using the Search input in the Audio pane, type the name of the ballad that we created in GarageBand.

If you forget what it sounded like, you can click the Play button and listen. If you're ready, click the Place at Playhead button. Wherever your playhead is at the time you click that button is where the song will start.

But that doesn't matter much, because we can slide the music to any point in the movie that we like. As you slide the music along the timeline, watch the Monitor above as it scrubs through the film. This helps us know where we want to put the music.

The ballad, if you recall, starts with a beat and a walking bass, and goes into piano. It's not harsh and doesn't have drama, so it won't really work with our first chapter. But if we place it in the second chapter, we might have something.

Slide the song to start just before the Island Life chapter marker.

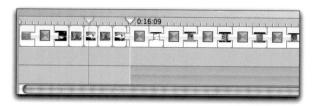

Play the movie. The drumbeat should start at about the point where the placard cross-fades into view.

The movie still starts out a little hollow. The first chapter needs something. But rather than use music, we'll apply sound effects.

In the Audio pane, click the pop-up menu that says iTunes Library, and scroll down to iMovie Sound Effects. You have two collections available out of the box: the Skywalker Sound Effects and the Standard Sound Effects.

Select Suspense from the Skywalker group. Put the playhead in the timeline at the beginning of the movie, and in the Audio pane, click the Place at Playhead button.

It fits. But It overlaps our ballad soundtrack. We can easily remedy this. We want to be able to control the volume of the soundtrack at very specific points in the movie, synchronizing it with specific images and actions.

Choose View > Show Clip Volume Levels (Command+Shift+L).

Two things occur. The most obvious is the purple line running through the soundtrack items. The second is the purple line that you'll notice in each transition you've created. You can ignore the volume lines in the transitions; they have no effect on what we have here. They work only if your clips and the transitions between them have audio already attached to them. iMovie lets you separate audio from video clips so that you can add your own or shift and dub them. In the case of our movie, however, the only audio present is the audio we've placed below the video, on the timeline.

And that audio, we can control. It works very much the same way that we controlled volume in the master track in GarageBand.

Click a point in the audio line. A small dot or sphere appears. That point allows you to change the volume up or down. So we can fade or increase the volume at very specific points that we can synchronize with video.

We want the Suspense sound effect only for the first chapter. We have two parallel audio tracks. If Suspense imported to the same track as the ballad, click and drag it to the empty track. With Suspense on its own track, it will be easier to manipulate. Click the purple volume line at a point just before the Island Life chapter marker (a small yellow diamond in the timeline).

Drag the point down to the bottom of the track. There. You've decreased the volume and created a fadeout for that sound effect.

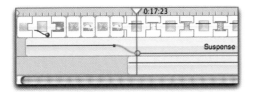

Preview the movie. The Suspense sound effect should help increase the drama of the storm and the rocks. The release from the suspense to the Island placard and the balladic music conveys the mood we want to evoke: that the island life is tranquil and inviting. We made lemonade from lemons. Or was it milk from coconuts?

The ballad carries us through the major part of the movie, but it doesn't reach the end. So we have to improvise. We could add more sound effects to round out the movie, or we could just overlap the ballad so that it matches the length of the film.

Let's opt for the overlap. This will show you another way to manipulate sound items in iMovie and exhibit the flexibility you have as a movie creator. Option-drag the ballad file to the right so that it overlaps about the length of two images. Then, using the volume control line, reduce the volume on the new duplicate until just after the overlap.

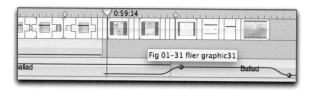

Test the film to make sure it works seamlessly. It may take some fidgeting, but it's not brain surgery.

We have completed a movie and told a story, using images, transitions, and soundtrack. Save the file.

We're not finished yet, however. Choose File > Share. In the ensuing dialog box, select QuickTime; then click Web in the pop-up menu . This way, we'll have a mini version of the movie that won't take too long to test. We'll make a full version shortly.

Let's take a second now to refer to our Rules of Thumb, particularly the character of our intended audience. As we pondered earlier, if the audience is a bunch of potential customers, we might choose one sound-track. If it's our grandparents, it may be quite another one altogether. Or not. But this is really an academic argument at this point. What we really want to think about is just how easy it is to create different movies from the same movie. That's not a riddle. We've experimented with different types of moods with our television set, with iTunes, and with an iPod (if we have one). We've seen how just changing the tune changes the point of view. Well, we've also made two distinct soundtracks for our movie. Let's put them to use.

As an alternative—and to exhibit using the very same images with a dif-ferent set of sound effects and soundtrack music—we can change our movie from one type of movie to a very different movie. Let's use the other GarageBand song we created as the background music.

So select the instances of the ballad, along with the Suspense sound effect, and delete them.

We'll start over with sound now. First, go to the Audio pane, and find the second GarageBand song you created. In the timeline, position the playhead at the Island Life chapter marker. In the Audio pane, click the Place at Playhead button. Once again, you'll see the song in the timeline.

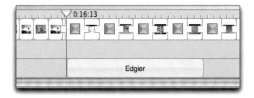

This song is much shorter than the first, so we'll be filling the movie with other sound effects and overlaying them to create an atmosphere.

The first thing we may want to do is extend our song along the middle part of the movie. We're fortunate in that we designed this edgier song so that it can loop itself without sounding as though it's starting over.

Option-drag the song across the timeline to make three duplicates. The song should now repeat from the first chapter marker right through to the end titles.

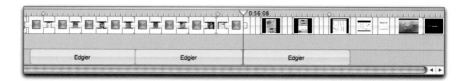

Before you go further, save the file, giving this version of the movie a unique name and its own identity. This will ensure that we don't write over our original ballad-based movie. Also, we will be able to compare our two movies when we're done adding sound.

Place the playhead at the beginning of the movie. In the Audio pane, go to the iMovie Sound Effects, and in Skywalker Sound Effects, select Boat Bell. Click the Place at Playhead button.

Keeping an eye on the timeline, drag the Boat Bell sound effect to the right, measuring to around 1 second after the beginning of the movie. The sound effect gives us only one bell, so duplicate it (Option-drag), and leave a little space between the duplicates. We want the foreboding to come from space this time. The low level of sound effects at the opening will contrast better with the insistent electronic beat of the music soundtrack in the next part of the movie.

We're still making *design decisions* every step we take.

Preview the first part of the movie.

Let's add another subtle piece of sound. In the Audio pane, find Cold Wind. Place it on the top sound track, starting at the opening of the movie.

We may need to add a third instance of the Boat Bell sound effect. The third toll adds drama.

Preview the movie again.

The edgy music comes in too quickly. We need a pause, with just the wind whistling. Again, this will heighten any drama we can muster before the edgy music.

There is one more thing we can do to raise the drama level. Let's insert a few seconds of emptiness just after the second images of the rocks...*before* we discover the island.

Make sure the timeline is in Time mode and not Clip mode. Select the transition after second rock image in the timeline, and delete the transition. Along with the transition, you may want to delete the Pier image; at this point, it doesn't add anything to the movie. Next, drag the next image over to the right for the space of 2 seconds. Check the interactive readout at the playhead.

The space we're providing will be black. The only thing that we'll hear at this point is the Cold Wind sound effect. Make sure that the music starts with the appearance of the Island placard. Make the adjustments to the sound by selecting all the music pieces (Shift-clicking) and shifting them to the right to align with the images.

Preview the movie.

The 1 or 2 seconds of black space countered by the start of the music gives us the drama we want. Now let's adjust the ending of the film's soundtrack.

Once again, choose View > Show Clip Volume Levels (Command+Shift+L). Scrub your timeline over to the last frames.

Create a fadeout for the music, just at the last frame of the business card. Now, for balance again, let's add the Cold Wind sound effect over the titles.

Save the file. Now let's make a proof of the movie so that we can compare the two movies and see the difference a soundtrack makes. Choose File > Share > QuickTime > Web.

It's interesting that even though the images are the same, the addition of two very different soundtracks changes the story.

So we should realize that the choice of soundtrack holds a lot of weight and can change the point of view of the whole movie.

By placing sound effects strategically, using blank screens and spacing, and mixing different soundtracks, we can take what is essentially raw material and bend it and shape it to form our own perspective, voice, or point of view.

Don't quit iMovie just yet. We'll be needing it in a moment.

Delivery

We have several options for the delivery of our movie. We could attach a video camera and send it to tape. We could burn a video CD, which works well enough in illegal black markets as a cheap way of viewing movies. Or we could burn a DVD, with menus, professional menu pages, scene selections, and all the other things we have come to expect from the format.

If your Macintosh is equipped with what Apple calls a SuperDrive, which lets you burn read and write CDs and DVDs, you'll be able to use iDVD. Otherwise, you will have to revert to exporting your video via QuickTime directly from within iMovie. Choose File > Share to choose the appropriate export method. The rest of us will move on to burning a DVD. Come along, if you care to, because this is interesting and easy nonetheless.

iDVD is a simple program if you let it be simple. It lets you use prefabricated themes, as Keynote and Pages do, to build the DVD user interface. But it can also be more complex than that, letting you design, apply, and customize your own themes; add and remove text; situate items; and use full-motion video.

You should still have iMovie open with your preferred movie active and saved. Click the iDVD Pane button. We have three chapter markers listed and one button we haven't used yet. Click the Create iDVD Project button to launch iDVD. One dialog box will open. Click the recommended Render and Proceed button.

We're now at a point of *design decision* again. It's at junctures when we're presented with what are seemingly mind-numbing choices that we really should take a few moments to consider our Rules of Thumb. "Who is the audience for this project?" is the first and most obvious question. But don't ask this question without first making available a design context. By that, I mean also consider what materials you now have in front of you. In this case, we're talking about the so-called custom themes in iDVD.

When we can answer "Who will be our audience?" in conjunction with "What do we have readily available to deliver it?", we can move forward with some conviction. And the answers to those questions sometimes don't come until we've dipped our toes into the pool.

Depending on which version of iDVD you have installed, the startup theme may differ. Your reflex action when you open iDVD should be to click the Customize button, which will open the important tool palette we're going to use.

Familiarize yourself with as many of the themes as you can. In one sense, these themes are to the video or DVD designer what fonts are to the print designer. The theme you choose will be another factor in the message you want to convey and how it comes across.

The themes that iDVD provides you are excellent starting points. In fact, they're excellent as finishing points, too. But there are times when you want to add your own touches, make them seamless, and still leverage the professional design quality of what the application provides you.

One thing to note, however, is that because we started iDVD directly from iMovie, we already have populated our Home menu with Play Movie and Scene Selections buttons. If you were to open iDVD on its own, the only thing you would have in your theme would be the title text, which you would replace with the title of your movie. It doesn't matter which theme you choose: If you've started iDVD from iMovie, you've saved yourself a few steps.

Also, be forewarned that the more complex the theme (meaning the more moving and sliding video components it has), the longer it takes to render. This is a factor to consider should you get the idea, half an hour before you have to rush out the door, that you'd like to bring a fresh new DVD along with you. You won't get it done in half an hour. Sure, this is cutting-edge technology, but our penchant for instant gratification only leads to heartache.

In designing anything under any deadline, there is yet another Rule of Thumb you should take to heart. Paste it, in fact, on your wall, or print it in reverse and pin it to the wall behind you so that when you are looking at yourself with the new iSight camera you've bought, you can have it right-reading.

And the words of wisdom are these:

> *You're in a hurry, so take your time.*

Add menus and themes

With that in mind, let's return to business at hand. To the right of the theme buttons are some other buttons that might interest you. Skip the Settings button for the moment, and click the Media button. When you're working with a prefab theme and don't want to bother customizing it much, you can, at the very least, choose the music loop you'll want to play on the initial menu screen of the DVD. This is where you do that.

Very similar to the way you do in iMovie, you can search and select directly from your iTunes collection.

The pop-up menu in the Media drawer also gives you direct access to your iPhoto library. Once again, you should notice the integration with the other iLife applications.

You can make an end run around any of these presets, of course, and go directly to the Finder, find the particular photo image, and drag it directly into the live theme window.

The same methods can be used for the Movie pop-up menu in the Media panel. If there's a movie that you haven't put in the Movies folder in your Home account on your Macintosh, one that lives somewhere buried deep in the Documents folder, you can easily find it and drag it to the hotspot area on the DVD theme and have it run its loop.

It's when you get to the nitty-gritty of setting up how your DVD menu page will play that you have to use a different drawer window.

So now return to the left one, stop, and click the Settings button. The Settings pane is divided into three sections. The Menu section gives you a space to choose not only your theme, but also the duration of time before the graphics and music end their loop and begin again.

This can be a critical aspect of how the menu presents itself, because with this control, you can match the exact duration of a song loop or the QuickTime movie you want it to show.

Further, you have more control of text styles, button styles, and placement. In other words, you can *design* your menu yourself.

As a test, drag any image from your hard disk into the Background thumbnail. Voilà. Your image is now your theme. All of a sudden, the possibilities open up before us. We could easily use any image we've used in the movie itself as the background for the basic menu page of the DVD. We can design and customize our DVD and use all the skills we've acquired through the rigorous out-of-the-box training we've endured, all leading to this very moment.

So let's get started, shall we?

First, let's use a prefab theme. For the sake of argument, we'll begin in the Themes pane and select Old Themes. Then choose GenY. It's a simple, abstract theme with a woody color tone. The theme is just this side of generic, but test it, and you'll find that its motion aspects make it interesting enough to be a *cool* holder for our *cool* movie.

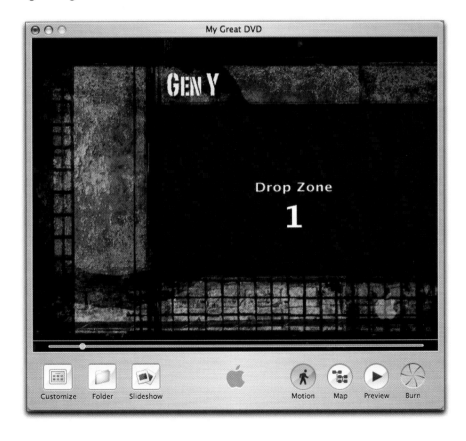

The title of the menu will match the title of the iMovie file. You can also change it. Out of the Box Island Life might be a nice title. Either way, we still have to fill in the drop zone, preferably with a scene of the iMovie. The chapter markers we made in iMovie have translated into scene selections. If you were to rent a DVD from the local movie-rental store, you'll inevitably find a scene-selection section on the DVD menu. And that is the same thing you've achieved, albeit on a rather smaller scale, in your DVD, using iMovie.

Click the Motion button at the bottom of the iDVD window. Because we made this whole movie not from video clips but from still images, we can choose what to fill the drop zone with. We can use one of the proof movies we made in iMovie and let it run through a few frames of transitions in the menu, or we can apply one of our still images and have that represent our movie. It will still animate, but will it work with our message well enough to satisfy the *compelling* factor we so desire? The easy way to find out is to test it.

Click your way back to iMovie. (Here's an easy way to get from application to application. Press Command + Tab, and then, while still holding down Command, tap the Tab key to step through a horizontal list of all your open applications. By the way, this is old-school Macintosh.) Put the timeline in Clip mode. Choose the Island placard from the timeline, and drag it directly onto the moving part of the theme. The yellow-and-black outline of the drop zone will appear, and your cursor will gain a green plus sign, telling you it's OK to drop the image in here.

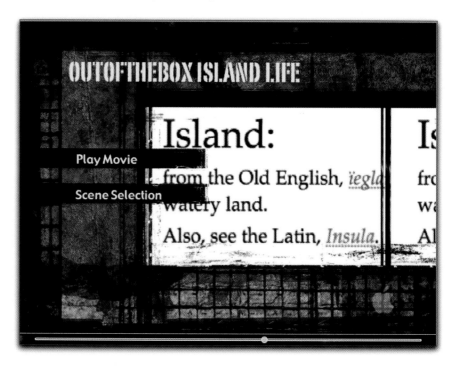

The single Island placard image tells enough and is dramatic enough to represent the whole film. If you feel there's an image that's better suited, all you have to do is replace the one you've just set there.

Or if you feel that the menu needs to have more movement than it already does, you can locate the small QuickTime proofs we made earlier and use them in the drop zone instead. You can drag them directly from the Finder, or you can locate them in the Media pane. It won't cost you anything more than time to experiment.

Remember that you must have the menu in motion when you drag to the drop zone. Otherwise, you're just adding data files to the DVD—which is another alternative. If you want to add the proof files to the DVD as extras, for example, turn Motion off, and drag the files from the Media pane directly to the menu. Instead of filling the drop zone, you'll automatically create a button that will link to the file.

iDVD has some other features, such as a built-in slideshow creator, but most of them don't pertain to the project at hand. One that does, however, is the Settings pane, which has customizing functions. Although the theme we've chosen works perfectly well, as emboldened designers, we can't resist playing around.

So you've set up the basic layout of the menu in the prefab design. We have another option at this point. Why not put our Print and Web projects on this DVD, as a sort of souvenir of our time in the islands? Remember, data is data, and a DVD can store a heck of a lot of it. All you have to do is put a new folder on the menu and fill it with your projects (Command+ Shift+N).

Now you want to change the size of the buttons and move their positions around the page. Open the Settings pane, and change the button from Snap to Grid to Free Position. Now select the button you want to move, and go to town. With the button selected, you can also define an animated transition for it. You should recognize the transitions from Keynote. Again, experiment, but keep simplicity as your watchword.

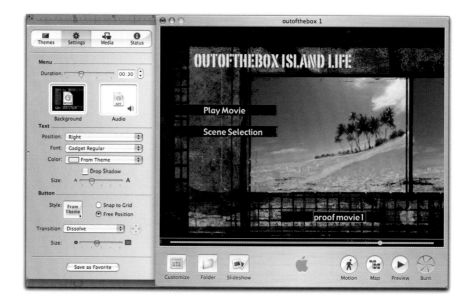

When you've decided that you've had enough, your audience is clamoring to see the movie, your design is clean, and the popcorn is starting to pop, click the Preview button to make sure. Walk your way through the DVD menu as you've set it up. It's a beautiful thing.

Insert a blank DVD disk, and click the Burn button.

All the pieces

All we had were a few images and a vague notion of making a movie. We started with several still images—some from screen grabs, some from the Web, and some from the Macintosh itself. We had no movement and no video footage. Let's face it—we had as near to nothin' as you'd ever want to see. And lo, through the power of our machine, the power of our resourcefulness, and the skills we acquired in previous chapters, we cobbled together a movie.

We've expanded the breadth of our skills into sound design. We took a sober look at the materials at hand and coerced them into a story. Finally, we delivered a story, with a point of view, in a format that could send it beyond the borders of our little room and out into the world.

There's only one thing left to do.

Do it again. And do it again after that. Find the shadowed nooks that you overlooked before, and shine a light on them. Introduce available technology, old and new, into your vision. And find your way to Carnegie Hall. You know how to do that, right?

Practice. Practice. Practice.

Chapter Four:
Hey, Joe, Whaddya Know?

4

Back in civilization, you can now purchase all the highfalutin software you want. But that doesn't mean you should forget all that you've learned through your previous out-of-the-box privation. If we catalog what we've created thus far, we'll see that we've done quite a bit. We have tools and skills that will help us survive in three distinct realms of design. We can design for print. We can design for the Web. And we can design for video. Within each of those fields, we've learned to use similar skills for different ends. And we've employed our Rules of Thumb as guidelines that don't dictate, but rather point a way through the forest of chaos to the clearing of design.

Here is a recap of what we've learned and a few basic guidelines to help you make good decisions about buying higher-end software when you take the next step into design.

Please send help.
We'll be running out
of inkjet ink soon.

Software Speculation: Print

●●●●●●

In the realm of print, we began by creating fliers. In so doing, we learned to balance a layout so that it not only says what you want it to say, but also shows it. We used image as text and text as image. We considered all elements on a page in both ways: as objects and as language.

The ability to view words on a page as both object and language lets us be more versatile. We're not bound by whatever mythical laws we were brought up to believe about type-means-message and pictures-mean-pretty. The pictures get upset when you tell them to just *sit in the corner, shut up, and look good.* Design doesn't have to be like a gangster's birthday party ("That's a nice flier…it would be a shame should somethin' happen to it").

In other words, no one is going to boss us around. Our design decisions will be based on what we know are the intentions of the piece, the expectations of the audience, and how we want that audience to read it.

From our fliers, we moved on to postcards. Our fliers and postcards are different but related pieces that expand our message or, in some cases, focus it. We've learned how to design postcards not only from a communications standpoint, but also from a somewhat technical production aspect. And this touches on some of the most important facets of design: technical skill and production knowledge.

Throughout this book, we've alluded to the technical side of design as we walked through each project. We didn't go into the technicalities of heavy-duty offset printing. But that doesn't excuse us from needing to know how it works if it becomes important to our work. Although we don't have to become experts in all the various aspects of printing, it's important for designers to understand enough of the process to make good design decisions.

The onus is on every designer to understand the process he or she is involved in. It's an ethic. Even though all architects don't have to know how to lay bricks or do finish carpentry, having a working knowledge of the basics is an essential part of being a professional in that field. The same is true with graphic design. Knowing the lay of the land lets you make efficient and profitable use of your time.

In that spirit, you have begun to understand the underpinnings of digital design through this book. By stripping away the high end and designing from what seemingly limited resources come only with your machine, you've had to rely on cunning and basic skills. And cunning and skills work. Business cards? Logos? You've done them.

The next steps into design will require more than just cunning. As you become more involved in design in the outside world, you'll start hearing terms like "workflow" and, even worse, "collaborative workflow." When this occurs, you can do one of two things:

- You can do your best impression of Edvard Munch's most famous painting, *The Scream,* and hightail it back to the deserted island.

- You can understand how the different design decisions you make on your projects fit into a particular workflow and how they can vary because of it.

Doing the first is easy. Practice first in front of a mirror. Doing the second is more involved. But there is a process and there are tools we can use to get there. You've already started. Beginning with the fliers, you had to make certain decisions about how to achieve certain objectives. Design is problem solving.

Look at the project in stages. First, take it in as a whole. Hold the idea at arm's length, and shift it in the light. Is it a flier? Is it a catalog? Is it an ad layout? Using the Rules of Thumb, figure out what your objective is and what medium best gets you there. Stranded on an island? Paper rolled up in a bottle. Simple. Look for the appropriate solution.

Next, consider the elements and parts you'll need to make it: images, fonts, colors, and space.

Finally, what applications or tools will we need to make it all happen? And here's where we go beyond just what came in the box. Sure, we know how to do the basics now, and we'll use these skills continually. But there are some things that you just can't do with AppleWorks and TextEdit. And that's when you need to bring in the big guns.

The right tools for the job

The most important application in any designer's kit is Adobe Photoshop. Photoshop is the premiere digital imaging application. It led the digital revolution in the late 1980s and has stayed on top of the heap ever since. Photoshop is now not just an application; it's a *verb*. It's become part of common parlance.

Knowledge of how to use it well, however, is not as common. Photoshop's learning curve is notoriously long. It can easily overwhelm you. But the way you approach learning the application's ins and outs can make all the difference. The big mistake most people make with Photoshop is trying to learn it by rote, all at once, or in all-in-one seminar sessions.

But after this book, you realize the fallacy of that approach. Of course you do.

Instead of trying to digest the mother of all digital imaging applications in one meal, by the book, so to speak, you'll better serve yourself by learning it through specific need.

And this goes directly to the methodology you've learned in this book. Start with the project. Start with the problem to be solved. Although Photoshop is not the easiest program to learn, if you concentrate on what you need to get done, you'll succeed. Along the way, you'll discover things both helpful and unnecessary. Always keep your original intention or vision in front of you. And err on the side of simplicity.

Here are some basics you should know about Photoshop.

Photoshop works in pixel-based images. Photos and images in Photoshop have specific resolutions. They are known as *raster images*. Among other things, if you increase the size of a raster image, you will lose some of its clarity. This relates directly to the printing process in particular. Offset printing relies on dots and screens. Ink on paper is finite and specific.

With printing, you must be concerned with how many dots per inch your images are, in what color space you create images, and at what line screen you're printing your project. Good design takes these things into account. And images created in Photoshop take these things into account.

One of the most powerful features to look for in any graphics application is which formats it outputs files to. This is true not only of Photoshop, but also of any program you use for making graphic elements and final pieces. In choosing applications to buy, this is a fundamental.

Photoshop exports images into virtually all of the relevant raster-based-image formats, such as TIFF, JPEG, GIF, and BMP. Each has its own merits and its specific use. For most print output, TIFF is best. JPEG is extremely popular, but it is based on what we call *lossy* compression. That means that when you save a file in JPEG, you are losing pieces of data, and the ensuing file will not be as high-quality as the original. JPEG is usually more suited for Web design. GIF is another Web-design file format.

But not all images and graphic elements are raster based. On the other side of the coin are what are known as *vector images.* Vector images rely not on resolutions and pixels but on mathematical formulas that define curves. Most of the time, the language of vector math is PostScript. Post-Script is a printer language developed by Adobe that interprets the curves, angles, and shapes of vector images onto the page. If you've ever seen a file with .eps at the end, you've encountered PostScript. *EPS* stands for *Encapsulated PostScript.*

You don't have to understand PostScript so long as you know that it is res-olution-independent. So you can resize a vector file at will and have no loss of quality. This is important when you're using illustrations. And the industry-standard program for vector art is also an Adobe program: Illustra-tor. There are other excellent vector art programs, such Macromedia Free-Hand, CorelDraw, and Deneba Canvas. But Illustrator is the one that you can be sure will be acceptable to all professional printers.

Illustrator's output formats rival those of its sibling, Photoshop. PDF, which we know is a great delivery format, is native to Illustrator. So anything you save as a native Illustrator file (.ai) will open in Adobe Reader, which is itself a free download and completely cross-platform (which means that it runs on the Mac and that other operating system people complain about).

Many students make the mistake of using Illustrator as a final delivery medium for their layout projects. Think of the program's name: Illustrator. Not Layout Maker. Not Brochureator. Not Catalogator. Illustrator. For illustrations.

But let's not blame the students. This mistake is not always their fault. For unknown reasons, graphic-design-school instructors often teach and pro-mote this practice, sending their poor-little-lamb students into the fero-cious world of design. The poor students bleat happily as they show their portfolios, filled with layouts designed and delivered in Illustrator. And they walk away jobless and confused.

Let's take away their confusion. Illustrator, like Photoshop, is for the *cre-ation* of elements, not necessarily their delivery in layout, just as a word processor is not a layout program, no matter what the templates and the online help application claims. If you are a student reading this, take heed. As you should realize by the end of this book, none of these applications exists in a design vacuum. That brings us back to the guideline suggested earlier in this chapter: Consider the whole of a project and then consider the parts you'll need to make it happen.

But don't get caught up in thinking that just one element or the program that helps you make it will work as the final presentation-and-delivery system of the project.

When it comes to layout, things get political. During the pre-Flood days of Mac OS 9, the preeminent layout program was QuarkXPress. In those days, the only other competitor for layout was PageMaker. But PageMaker was slow in its beginnings to separate and handle color printing properly. QuarkXPress, however, handled color wonderfully. And it had a modular and extensible, or scalable, architecture, letting you add specific tools to help you with specific design or output tasks. These so called XTensions became a cottage industry. Companies cropped up that specialized in XTension development. There were XTensions for creating drop shadows; for using layers; for working with variable data; for extending your artboard; and for meeting other very particular, very specific needs. They still exist.

For these reasons, QuarkXPress still exists. PageMaker, while still in existence, isn't available for Mac OS X. But we're 21st-century beings here. Thus, we have a better option than either of those two. We recommend Adobe InDesign.

Now, you may think we're shilling for Adobe here. After all, we've recommended three of its flagship applications. But our reasoning has little to do with the maker and much to do with the application-suite integration and functionality.

QuarkXPress was late in its transition to Mac OS X, and in that yearlong period, Adobe InDesign built its experience and honed its feature set to leapfrog its competition. QuarkXPress's interface hasn't changed much in the meantime, and its feature set hasn't convinced us that it's a modern, forward-looking application. Once again, integration with other high-end graphics applications makes a program's value soar. The integration with Photoshop and Illustrator makes InDesign superior.

We also have to look at the output format, of course. InDesign is built with PDF specifically in mind as its primary output format. So InDesign matches our method of design creation, with our focus on integration of applications and the delivery of your product in a near-universal format—PDF out of the box, as it were. QuarkXPress has a less-than-native output to PDF.

In the exercises in this book, you've experienced what it's like to work with programs that are well integrated and with programs that aren't. In the latter camp, recall what it was like moving from AppleWorks to iPhoto to TextEdit while assembling our print and Web documents. The commands we used in one program were different from those in the others—as were the toolbars, menus, and palettes where we chose those commands. Compare that with the experience of working with the iLife programs— iPhoto, iMovie, and GarageBand—to make our video. Think about how easy it was to browse iPhoto images from iMovie, and think about how Garage-Band's ability to export songs to iTunes made our movie score available from within iMovie without even having to launch iTunes itself.

When programs aren't tightly integrated, you can still get work done. But it sure is a lot easier when applications work together out of the box.

Learn from experts

It's also important, in design and the design workflow, to have a knowl-edgeable printer (the person who prints, not the machine) to walk you through the printing process. A little knowledge can take you a long way. Never be afraid to ask questions of professionals you come across. Print-ers, color retouchers, and photographers may not have a complete knowl-edge of your workflow, but their expertise in their particular areas can give you a greater understanding of your own part, as well as of the overall process.

Knowledge is power, especially knowing how to save time and money by using the tools you have in front of you or by using the expert skills of those around you.

When you're looking for programs to help you do all the kinds of work we did out of the box, don't look for an all-in-one solution. Although it may seem to be the best route—the most efficient method is to go for a one-stop shop—you might also find it limiting. Rather than put all the function-ality into one do-it-all application, high-end software developers tend to keep their applications focused on specific areas. Then they integrate the parts of the applications that need relationships. This compartmentalizing actually helps you create better design and make better design decisions. Think about it: Each part of your layout has its own stand-alone integrity, but each also has an integral relationship with the other parts. Once again, we're looking at the layout as a conversation between elements.

These days, the best software for design is often bundled in suites, with clearly defined application functions and well-integrated interfaces and out-puts. We're a long way out of the box at this point. The applications we're recommending are often more than just a *few* bucks more. But looking at the whole what-to-buy conundrum with an eye toward economics in the overall long term might make software applications seem less expensive and more valuable to you at the same time. Businesspeople call it *ROI,* or *return on investment.*

They love those acronyms (or should we say TLTA?). One businessman said that to me recently. He said, "Your design software seems expensive to me, but I suppose you get a good ROI." I was savvy and nodded, having to think for a moment ("Oh, yeah. Return on investment").

Software Speculation: Web

What do we know about Web design? Well, we know that it's very different from designing for print. The file formats, the layouts, the speed, and the colors all work differently.

The limitations and compromises you find in any kind of design, you find threefold in Web design. But there are some applications out there that try their best to minimize that aspect of Web development.

What you find when you enter the world of Web design is that proportionally, there's more of Web and less of design—at least, at first glance. You'll have to familiarize yourself with more computer terminology. In fact, you'll probably say words like *terminology* instead of opting for the simpler version *term*, as in *computer terms.* Web work does that to you. Your voice won't become more nasal, and your pant legs won't necessarily rise above your ankles (unless acted on by some outside force, like hot-water washing), but you may notice that your bathing habits might change. Be forewarned. When you enter the big world of Web design, you'll be unleashing the inner geek to one degree or another.

There are many choices for Web designers just starting out. The first and most obvious for us Macintosh users is, of course, .Mac. As we discussed in Chapter 2, a .Mac. account is certainly the easiest way to send content up on the Web. It doesn't actually give you your own domain name; neither does it serve as such for anyone who might want you to design her own domain. But as a sort of way station, personally or designwise, it works out fine.

The Public folder of your iDisk is an excellent FTP site. (You remember that *FTP* means *File Transfer Protocol,* as opposed to Hypertext Transfer

Protocol, or HTTP.) An FTP site can be used as an alternative to email attachments. Most email servers, for example, have a size limit that gets in the way of sending massive amounts of documents. But with an FTP account, you can put files online, limiting who has access by way of passwords, and know your specific space limits. There are many shareware and freeware FTP clients, which is a geeky way of saying "mini FTP applications that do just file transfer." FTP file transfers are also faster than using email downloads or going through a browser.

But as we go farther along and want to design our own pages, set up our own domains, and design for others in turn, we have to look beyond the box we've been living in up to this point.

But let's set up some criteria first to help make any purchase decisions, just as we would design decisions. First of all, if we want to come at it from a designer's standpoint, we should look for applications that orient from that perspective as well. Don't get your hopes up too much, however. There really is no escape from having a working knowledge of HTML. You don't have to know enough to create it so long as you can read it, even at a Dick-and-Jane level.

No app is an island

The first thing to look for, then, is a WYSIWYG editor. That's more geeks-peak for a what-you-see-is-what-you-get program. There are three excellent WYSIWYG applications for the Mac, and none of them is from Microsoft. Yet.

The three are Macromedia Dreamweaver, Adobe GoLive, and Softpress Freeway. These three are all WYSIWYG, and they all cater, in some fashion, to designer *and* geek. Each of these is the layout and delivery application, similar in general function to InDesign or QuarkXPress in print. They don't make the doughnuts, but they lay them out nicely in the tray.

Dreamweaver is the premier Web-design application. In simple terms, Dreamweaver is akin to InDesign in its function. It's the playing field, the delivery system, the layout app. But in Web design, it's still not that simple, because you can't do any image editing in Dreamweaver. You can create a lot of the interactivity, the page positioning and layout, and much of the look and feel, but you can't make the images to any great degree. You need digital imaging applications.

The first digital imaging application to come to mind is, of course, Photoshop. And many people opt for that because it's the only one they know so far, because it's the only one we've mentioned in this chapter so far, and because these applications are relatively expensive and we can't afford to buy another.

Image-editing alternatives

But it is not the only one out there in the world. Although Photoshop is the mother of all digital imaging applications, it is not necessarily the best one for every job. Before you turn away, calling me a blasphemer, open your heart to Macromedia Fireworks. Fireworks is the Photoshop for the Web. Let's not deny that Photoshop has Web-specific features. But even it has a mini application called ImageReady that handles its Web work for it. Photoshop was originally designed for print, and it does that with no rivals. But it does seem to be less agile when it's used for the Web.

In the same way that Photoshop, InDesign, and Illustrator work together as an application suite (in fact, they're part of Adobe Creative Suite 2, or CS2 for short), Dreamweaver, Fireworks, and Flash are part of Macrome-dia's Studio 8 suite.

The Studio 8 suite has the integration among applications that we crave. Each application is a robust stand-alone program. But when combined with its suite siblings, each application becomes greater than its isolated self. In fact, it's arguable that Macromedia's suite model predated the Adobe CS model.

The reciprocity between Dreamweaver and Fireworks is known in their marketing lingo as Roundtrip HTML. That means that changes you make in one application are available to you, updated, when you switch to the other. And working in Dreamweaver and Fireworks together means you will be switching back and forth several times.

Fireworks is excellent for drawing out your page design. You can create your rollovers, swapping images, pop-up menus, and many of the other higher-function Web design doohickeys within Fireworks. You refine the effects and interactivity in Dreamweaver and create the Web-site structure in Dreamweaver. But Fireworks handles the design effects and the basic shape of home pages, in particular, and subsequent pages subsequently. Fireworks also creates your incidental graphics, repeating items, naviga-tion bars, and color palette.

Dreamweaver and Fireworks work in tandem, tag-team style. You can add to these two FreeHand, which is not part of the suite but is available sepa-rately from Macromedia. FreeHand started as a competitor to Illustrator for print design. But after seven versions, FreeHand shifted its focus to the Web and to integration with the Dreamweaver/Fireworks team. You *could* get by mixing and matching Dreamweaver, Photoshop, ImageReady, FreeHand, and Illustrator. But when you cross-pollinate your production this way, you lose some degree of efficiency.

But if there's one thing we've learned in this book, it's that you can cross-pollinate with applications, and sometimes, you find those happy accidents that take your design beyond your original intentions.

While we're talking about the Studio suite, we have to mention Flash. Flash is outside normal Web design. Think of it as an interactive animation creator. It has its own learning curve and its own rules. And though you can deliver Flash in its native format, directly on the Web, it's best to use Dreamweaver as the delivery system.

If your .swf files (the output format for Flash) constitute the entrée, Dreamweaver and HTML are the plates you serve them on.

Flash creates Web animations with music, motion, and interactivity, all the while keeping file sizes small. Bandwidth and throughput are among the other compromises you have to consider in Web design. But Flash sneaks past a lot of the more mundane problems of streaming video with its own use of vector graphics and automatic streaming. Oftentimes, it's easier and more efficient to make a file with sound in it in Flash. And Flash works with Dreamweaver in a reciprocal manner similar to Fireworks and Dreamweaver.

Designing in Flash is a unique combination of Web design and design for video. You have all the basic components of video—image, sound, and motion—and you have the added Web features of interactivity. The story is the subject of the Web site, and the point of view is altered by the interactivity available. Flash really does allow for full-on moviemaking, in a different delivery medium. But with all the great moviemaking features, you also have the limitations of the Web: file size, colors, and length of audience interest.

It is still rare for designers who know Flash to be proficient in other design applications. This could be because Flash takes a particular concentration and focus. But it may also be because designers may not understand that all design is design. The language of design is the same, no matter what the discipline is. Design is language. And disciplines are merely dialects.

It shouldn't be so rare to be able to design and work successfully in more than one digital medium. Once again, we have to look at our Rules of Thumb and make decisions accordingly.

Even more Web-design choices

And speaking of choices, we're not limited to the Macromedia suite for Web design. Among our other choices for Web design is Adobe GoLive. GoLive is part of the Adobe Creative Suite (starting to see a pattern here with all these suites?). Although it's not our favorite Web-design application, it too has quite a few features to recommend it. Among those features, GoLive works with Photoshop, ImageReady, and Illustrator, using what Adobe calls 360° HTML. Sounds familiar, doesn't it? Sort of like Roundtrip HTML. You have to wonder sometimes about those marketing professionals.

GoLive led the way in professional-level WYSIWYG Web design. Its original moniker was CyberStudio, and GoLive was the German company that developed it. It revolutionized the Web-design industry, which up to that point was populated by code writers and design dabblers. The best WYSIWYG available in the mid-1990s was Adobe PageMill. And though that may claim to be among the first design-oriented Web applications, its level of sophistication was not very high. Other applications were available, but GoLive CyberStudio put them all to shame with its sophistication and its insistence not on Web-*page* design but on Web-*site* design and management.

GoLive's interface is in line with those of its Creative Suite brethren, and it's reciprocity is almost up to speed with the Macromedia Dreamweaver/Fireworks roundtrip. Deciding which to opt for almost becomes an impulse rather than a preference.

When Adobe acquired GoLive, it brought it into the big leagues of software management and has continued to support it. GoLive is still around because of that support and because it has a large user base that swears by it. Now that Adobe has acquired Macromedia, the choices of Web development and design could go either way. But we have to recognize that because of the two companies' close rivalry, the acquisition of Dreamweaver by Adobe may open possibilities rather than decrease our choices. Time will tell. And this speculation and recommendation may date this book. So keep this book as a time capsule.

Softpress Freeway takes on the challenge of Web design from a print-design starting point. This software application is more akin to QuarkXPress or InDesign in its layout capabilities than it is to a traditional Web-design application. It does much of its code production—the heart of Web development—behind the scenes. It lets you concentrate on the design of your project rather than worry about the code.

This is a double-edged sword. For the dilettante designer, dabbling in Web design, it may work fine, but when push comes to click, you may be better served by learning basic HTML and some JavaScript.

The thing to remember when choosing a Web-design application is to look for how it works with the way *you* tend to work and then recognize how you can adapt your way of working to allow for integration of other applications. Improvisation and consideration of the project goals are integral parts of real design work, not the prescribed methods that software developers tell you are best. We called it compromise, but we might just as well call it a balancing act between what you or your project insists on and what's feasible.

We're no longer on an island, isolated and alone. From this point on, our work has to conform or at least converse with workflows larger than our own. Ask not for whom the mouse clicks. It clicks for thee.

Software Speculation: Video Production

When we began our video projects, we considered the three essential, perhaps more technical, components for movie production: image, sound, and motion. We also talked about the more ethereal and mercurial components you need: story and point of view.

Video production, perhaps more than either of the other two design fields of print and Web, relies on a larger outsourcing of skills. It's remarkable that just from within the box and the bundle that comes with your Mac, you can create professional- and broadcast-quality video and movies, with sound, movement, and story. We used the iLife application suite without even touching a video camera. From iPhoto to GarageBand to iMovie and iDVD, our work flowed through the integrated applications with a singular intention of making a movie. But we could have stopped at any point and used iPhoto for a quick slideshow solution. Or we could have fallen into the gaping black hole of GarageBand, getting lost in the possibilities of composing music from scratch.

We never really leave these applications behind, even in the higher end. We'll still use iPhoto for storyboard, and GarageBand is a pretty good way of composing soundtracks. But when you want to take the next step and get serious about it, you'll have to spend a little time learning some technical stuff.

Just knowing the terms *pan* and *zoom* won't make it—not until you've established yourself, that is. Then you can direct your cinematographer to tell the cameraman to pan across the set and zoom using his 24mm. All you need then are a monocle, some jodhpurs, and a riding crop. But to get to that point, you'll have to do some due diligence.

The move upward into that realm is a staged process. And to make that great first step from iMovie to the big time, you'll want to look at Apple Final Cut Express. (By the way, it pains us to say that iMovie isn't bigtime. You can probably stay with iMovie and make a feature film too—as long as you have a great story and a firm point of view.)

Final Cut Express is a phenomenal application. It's professional-level video production with an easier interface and not so long a learning curve. It's also relatively cheap. It will take you beyond the drag-and-drop Ken Burns Effect world of iMovie into the more sophisticated universe of filmmaking with effects, with true-to-the-frame timelines and better-than-QuickTime output.

But more important, it is like a film university's second-semester moviemaking class. The principles remain the same, but the tools and the story making become more complex. Remember, again, that design is language. Video and film are other dialects, not groups of incomprehensible foreign symbols. Just the simple Rules of Thumb that you learned to consider in Chapter 1 carry over into every aspect of expression in design.

GarageBand also has its more sophisticated cousins. Apple Soundtrack and Logic, and Digidesign ProTools, fall in line with Apple Final Cut Pro, Motion, and Shake, and Adobe After Effects. If you're already working in sound design, you may have other favorites. But don't discount GarageBand as just kid stuff. Simplicity in design works just as well in music and sound.

Our tools become more complex as our intentions do. Final Cut Express is the stepping-off point to Final Cut Pro. And from Final Cut Pro, the digital filmmaking world opens into effects. Other applications come to the fore: Adobe After Effects and Apple's Shake and Motion. Still, don't forget Photoshop. It peeks around the corner into every part of digital design.

With Apple's professional suite, you can begin compositing video, compositing effects, and composing films. Again, the tools are complex, but the principles remain the same. At the heart of all these high-end application suites lie two things: simplicity and clear intent.

Leave the Piano Where It Is

At the beginning of this book, I told you that you didn't want to be a designer. It's too much trouble; there are too many demands for your opinion. You're forever moving furniture, be it in the room, or in your head, or just on the page. Well, I have some bad news for you: You can't escape being a designer. Everyone who uses language is a designer. Forming words is an act of design.

We're all designers, but not to the same degree. The degree to which we are designers is the degree to which we can recognize and decipher the designs around us.

If you've ever set a table, you've created design. It's not necessarily art, and it's not necessarily commercial, but it is design. Design is moving something from an existing state to a preferred one. Don't tell your teenagers to clean their rooms. Have them redesign it to your preferred state of clean. Redesign the mess. See, it's functional, too.

We're all like tourists in a foreign country. At first, we can't speak the language. The signs tell us nothing, and the sounds we hear are strange. The words are unfamiliar, and we have to point at what we want, like children. After a while, however, we start to pick things up. Words that were once unrecognizable now begin to make sense and gain meaning to us.

As we start to learn the language of this foreign place, it begins to be less foreign. We know where to turn right and where to go straight. We see the address numbers, and they make sense. The map is readable.

Well, design is like that. When we begin to speak the language of design, we start to understand how the various and previously unintelligible forms combine to show intention and meaning. We begin to take control, to take ownership of our surroundings.

Here's our final exercise. You don't have to bring your Macintosh, but if you have a laptop, feel free. Walk around your block. Choose three houses or three buildings within one block. Try to read the architecture of each building as though it were a flier describing itself. Each building should argue its point and give you a call to action: to enter, walk by, or simply admire. Believe me, the architect had these decisions in mind when he or she was designing it.

When you've discovered the language of the block, take photos. Make a short film, expressing the argument and the story of the architecture of that block. Make a flier. Design.

Consider your own house or building now. As you enter, make yourself aware of the layout, the colors, and the headline of the entryway. Walk through the house, and make yourself aware of the argument and the language of the wall colors, the furniture layout, the usability.

These are all design considerations, and they do affect us. The more we are aware of them, the better we can change them to suit our own lives. We can redesign them. We can own the decisions we make. Where does the couch go? What about the piano?

As our fluency in the language of design increases, we empower our own use of our tools and our language. We can play on the words; we can make our intentions known.

The bottom line is your Macintosh. Your Macintosh is your design Rosetta stone. It helps you take the seemingly incomprehensible, disparate worlds of digital expression—from print to Web to video and audio—and make them make sense to you. You can read! But more important, you can write, too. You can etch your vision, your point of view, your dire need of expression or rescue with one machine. You know which screw to turn, and how much, and maybe even when. It all begins with language—and that, my fellow designers, is where it finally comes to rest.

Index